Table of Co

Introduction... 1

Doctrine of Sound Words 3

Dictionary in Alphabetical Order............................. 7

Postmodern Words.. 111

Theological Terms in Layman Language

The Doctrine of Sound Words

Martin Murphy

Second Edition

To my wife Mary
The reason for publishing this work
With love

Introduction

I have read hundreds of books relative to Christian doctrine and theology over the past thirty-five years. The number of lectures and sermons are innumerable. During that time, hundreds of theological words, terms, and concepts were unknown to me. I started collecting a list of unfamiliar words and defining them based on my understanding of that particular topic or in the case of a person at least a brief study of his life and work. The goal was to keep the terms in layman friendly language. This work began, and as it remains in progress, every attempt has been made to keep the definitions as objective as possible.

The terms and phrases are in alphabetical order. The relationships with other terms are indicated by using brackets [ ] at the end of the definition. Greek, Latin words and phrases are often used in theological and doctrinal writings. When a Greek or Latin word is defined, the actual translation to English immediately follows the Greek or Latin word in parentheses ( ).

Although many of these terms are commonly known, this brief work is based on my understanding of the classical meaning. The student may benefit by simply perusing the content. I hope this will help Christians better understand the nature and character of God.

Doctrine of Sound Words

The Equivocation of Language is the result of misusing words. The principle denigrates the proper use of the language in our culture. The intentional effort to equivocate language has been with us since the fall of the human race. In fact, deceit was one of the causal factors in the fall. It was the father of deception that said to Eve, "Has God indeed said..." (Genesis 3:1). From Adam and Eve to the last baby born, there will always be the twisting of language. The Sophists of the 5th century B.C. were famous for turning philosophical skepticism into the impossibility of absolute knowledge, which in essence denies absolute truth.

The biblical doctrine of sound words is necessary to avoid the equivocation of language. "Hold fast the pattern of sounds words which you have heard from me..."(2 Timothy 1:13). I translate it from the Greek text in terms of having an outline of healthy words. There are three parts to this short phrase from the Bible. The command is have or to hold fast. The pattern refers to a summary account or an outline of sound words. Sound words are healthy words which provide good health for the soul

Unfortunately, worldly passions lead to words of confusion and words of strife rather than sound words. The result is forgotten doctrine. But aside from what I call necessary forgotten doctrine, The following simple principles have not been taught:

Human beings are born sinful creatures.
Human beings deserve eternal damnation and punishment.
God is longsuffering, compassionate, and merciful.
Call on God for today is the day of salvation.

If sound words have been taught, why do Christians misunderstand these simple concepts? If sound doctrine has been taught why do so many professing Christians believe that sinful man can save himself? These questions should not be taken lightly. A summary of the sound words from God imprinted on the souls of men, women, boys and girls would eliminate these questions.

A summary of sound words is not equal to quoting Bible verses. It has often been said that biblical texts may be found to prove almost anything. Unbelievers, liberals, the ignorant and scholars use Bible verses taken out of context to prove their opinions. One Bible verse does not equal the entire Word of God. The whole counsel of God must be in agreement.

 The goal of every Christian should be to gather a summary of the Word of God so that God is exalted and man is put down. For instance, the doctrine of God must be relative to God's nature and the doctrine of man must be relative to man's nature. When we hold fast to the healthy words of Scripture we will save ourselves and our progeny from theological error.

Error in doctrine will inevitably lead to error in practice. When a man believes wrongly, he will act wrongly. The very cause of division, schism, quarrels, and bickering in the church is a result of wrong teaching. Why? Because, Christians have ignored the outline of healthy words from Scripture

Christians cannot hold fast to something unless they understand it. The task is not easy, but it is necessary. God's people are custodians of God's truth and they must hold fast to His truth in faith and love.

Christians must not only leave a summary of the Christian religion to the coming generations, they must hold on to that summary of the Christian religion by the power of the Holy Spirit so they will have reasons to believe.

It was the use and misuse of words that compelled me to write *Theological Terms in Layman Language.*

Dictionary in Alphabetical Order

Achilles Heel of Christianity. In Greek mythology Achilles was the greatest of the Greek warriors in the Trojan War, but was mortally wounded in the heel. So it is said that the vulnerable point in the Christian religion, or the "Achille's heel" is the alleged "problem of evil." In reality, there is no weakness in the Christian religion, but Christians must have a sound biblical theodicy to refute the enemies of Christianity. [See Theodicy; Mystery]

Active obedience. Christ voluntarily entered into the covenant of redemption with God the Father and was absolutely obedient to the law of God. The active obedience of Christ was not merely his sufferings in His life and death, but obeying the perfect requirements of the law. Christ fulfilled the ceremonial, judicial, and moral law, so that those who are in Christ can be said to be obedient to the whole law through the act of justification. [See Romans 5:19 and Philippians 2:8]

Actus forensis. (the actualization of a legal state) This is the Protestant concept of justification. Christians are declared righteous in Christ which makes them righteous while in themselves they remain sinners. Martin Luther said the redeemed are *simul justus et peccator* which means "at the same time sinner and just." Legally Christians are declared righteous in the sight of God, but morally they retain a remnant of the sinful nature until glorification. [See Justification]

Actus physicus. (the actualization of a physical state) The concept of justification according to the Roman Catholic Church. It refers to an infusion of grace that makes one righteous in him or herself. Protestants tend to err by believing that the goodness and virtue of Christ is placed within the heart. God does not make a person righteous. God declares a person righteous. [See Justification]

Ad fontes. (to the sources) A Latin term popularized during the Italian Renaissance (1350 A.D. – 1425 A.D.). It was a call to return to the classics and writings of the ancient Greek and Roman literature. For Christians of every generation, the war cry ought to be "return to the original sources" which is the Word of God.

Adonai. The Hebrew word translated in the New Testament as Lord translated from the Greek word *kurios*. This was the highest title attributed to God. It communicates absolute authority over a dependent creation from an independent Being. [See Kurios/kurion]

Agents of Revelation. God uses humans as agents of revelation, men who communicate God's word to God's people. They were known as prophets in the Old Testament and Apostles in the New Testament. One of the marks of the agent of revelation was his seeing God perform miracles, which attest to his authority. [Matthew 9:1-8]

Allegory. In biblical interpretation, the interpreter seeks to find a "deeper" or "spiritual" meaning in a text. The Greek word *allegoria* may be literally translated as "speaking one thing, but signifying something else." The allegorical concept is explicitly found in Galatians 4:24 where Paul speaks allegorically saying: "for these women are two covenants, one proceeding from Mount Sinai bearing children who are to be slaves; she is Hagar." The misuse of the allegorical method is common and leads to multiple meanings of Scripture. The allegorical method should be used with the greatest of care with the most skilled of godly men engaged in the interpretation of Scripture. [See Grammatico-Historical; Hermeneutics]

Alms giving. According to the Roman Catholic Church it is a work of satisfaction which is seen as a means of grace. It involves giving money to the church and/or the needy. It is a legitimate biblical doctrine as the Scripture so clearly teaches "it is more blessed to give than to receive" however it is not a means of grace. (Acts 20:25)

Amillennialism. The term technically implies "no millennium." The clear teaching of Scripture states that there is a millennium. The most prominent text relative to millennialism is Revelation 20:1-10. Although there are various views from amillennialists, many of them do not believe the one thousand years mentioned in Revelation 20 refers to a literal one thousand year reign between Christ's first and second comings. Therefore, the one thousand years refers to a long period of time prior to the second coming of Christ and the final judgment.

Analogy of faith. This is the foundation for biblical interpretation according to the 16th century Reformers. It states that difficult passages of Scripture must be interpreted in light of other clear passages. This fundamental principle of the sixteenth century Reformation acknowledges "Scripture alone" as the basic doctrine of Protestant Christianity. The rejection of "Scripture alone" was the primary irresolvable division between the Roman Catholic Church and the Protestant Church. [See Sola scriptura]

Analogia entis. (the analogy of being) A term introduced by Thomas Aquinas which means there is a point of contact between the infinite and the finite or some similarity between God and man. (i.e. - God has a sovereign will, man has a non-sovereign will. The similarity is that both have wills, but of a different nature). Protestants generally reject this Thomistic approach and its arguments of the principle of analogy between the Creator and the creature based on natural reason. However, some Protestant theologians like James Henley Thornwell believed that "[R]eason is so constructed that as soon as it cognizes any being, it must cognize God. The inference from one to the other is immediate, intuitive, and necessary." The process of reasoning by analogy must be based on real properties to make the comparison more or less intelligent. [See Reason]

Analytical justification. Under scrutiny God finds a person to be just. This is the Roman Catholic view that God will declare a person righteous only if they are actually, or by analysis, righteous. Therefore they must cooperate with the infused grace poured into the soul in order to produce a real personal righteousness. [See Justification]

Animism. The belief that an individual spirit resides in anything, either animate or inanimate. This was the beginning point for the historical critical school because they believed religious thought in history moved from the simple to the complex and that animism was a very primitive religion.

Annihilationism. A theory, almost unknown to Christianity until recent history, that teaches the souls of unbelievers cease to exist in the future life. It is unclear as to when annihilation will occur. Several prominent evangelical theologians have adopted and developed this doctrine which also means a denial of the literal existence of Hell. Dr. John Gerstner wrote a book entitled "Repent or Perish" to annihilate the annihilation theory. The logical end of this theory is universalism. [See Universalism]

Anthropology. The study of human existence. Although it is a category to itself, this theological discipline begins with the origin of human beings and encompasses their progressive development in redemptive and world history.

Anthropomorphic language. When used in biblical interpretation, it uses human characteristics to denote something about God. For example when Job said "Pity me, pity me, O you my friends, For the hand of God has struck me" (Job 19:21) the word "hand" does not refer to a hand like a human hand because God does not have a body. God's hand is a symbol of power over the creature. [See Hermeneutics]

Antilegomena. This refers to the New Testament books disputed by some in the early church. Hebrews, James, 2 Peter, 2 and 3 John, Jude, and Revelation, were some of those disputed books. [See Canon]

Antinomianism. The world and life view that is opposed to keeping the law of God. Reformed churches teach that Christians have the responsibility to keep the law of God, but because of the remnant of the sin nature, Christians never perfectly keep God's law. [See Law of God]

Antinomy. (against law) The mutual contradiction of two principles resting on premises of equal validity. This is against the law of non-contradiction. It literally means "against the word" or "against law." Christians use this term to try and satisfy their minds when a contradiction appears. [See Law of non-contradiction]

Antithesis. The opposite of thesis. Hegel's dialectical idealism teaches that an idea or proposition provokes an opposing idea in a dialogue, and that these two ideas join to create a synthesis, which becomes a new thesis, that provokes an antithesis, *ad infinitum*. [See Hegel]

Apartheid. (for theological purposes this word refers to being apart) In theology this refers to apartness with reference to God's transcendence. Although God is above creation, He is not removed from creation. This is not to be confused with regard to human segregation. [See Transcendence; Immanence]

A priori knowledge. (from the former) This is innate immediate knowledge. It is built in before sense experience. It is associated with causality based on the assumption that the sufficient cause is *a priori* to the effect. The apostle Paul ways "what may be known of God is manifest in them" (Romans 1:19) and that the "law of God is written in the hearts of all men" (Romans 2:15).

A posteriori knowledge. (from the latter) This knowledge gained through induction or deduction. With respect to apologetics it is a term applied to those proofs for the existence of God that begin with the finite order and ascend toward the first cause.

Apologetics. The discipline of presenting claims to first prove theism and then presenting claims to prove various aspects of the Christian faith. Apologetics is commanded for many reasons including aiding in the following five dimensions:

1) obey Scripture
2) stop the mouth of the noisy contenders
3) common grace considerations
4) strengthen believers
5) pre-cvangclism value

The normative for Christian apologetics is found in the life and ministry of the apostle Paul. It was his practice to reason with Jews and God-fear Gentiles (Acts 17:17). [See Classical apologetics; Presuppositional apologetics]

Apotheosis. This term refers to the deification of man. This is not the same as the Greeks and Romans treating men and gods equally. It refers to professing Christians calling themselves god in terms of the triune God of the Bible. It begins with the idea that man has a spark of divinity within himself or herself. Liberal theologians use the concept relative to the immanence of God and the fact that the soul of man and its composition is the spark of divinity. [See Immanence]

Aquinas, Thomas. A Roman Catholic theologian, apologist, and philosopher of the 13th century. His work on natural revelation, natural reasoning and especially the law of causality has earned him a place in the historical hall of fame. He distinguished between nature and grace in order to argue for their harmony.

Argumentum ad baculum. (to the stick) An informal fallacy in logical argumentation that is no more than an argument by intimidation. The strength of the argument is on the basis of "might makes right." For example, your proposition is false because I'll hit you if you disagree. The appeal to force to validate the truth is an invalid way to argue a proposition.

Argumentum ad fontes. (to the sources) Erasmus used this term as a call to return to the original Greek or the original sources to understand Christian doctrine and theology. Christians have a responsibility to consult original sources as much as possible to confirm a doctrine or some other belief system. For example a church historian may interpret a historical event so that when it is reported it is not consistent with the original event or doctrine.

Argumentum ad hominem abusive. The ad hominem (to the man) argument is an informal fallacy where the opponent attacks the man rather than the argument. For example, your proposition is false because you are ugly.

Argumentum ad misericordiam. (to pity) This is an informal fallacy where the opponent appeals to pity in the argument. For example, your proposition is false because I've had a bad day and never get to win an argument.

Argumentum ad populum. (to the people) An informal fallacy where the opponent appeals to the multitude to win his argument. For example, evolution must be true because the majority of people believe it.

Argumentum ad verecundiam. (to modesty) An informal fallacy where the opponent appeals to authority. For example, your proposition is false because Dr. Sagan disagrees with you. It is appropriate to appeal to some recognized authority in a particular field, but the argument must stand on its own merit.

Arianism. This view denied that Christ was co-essential, co-eternal, or consubstantial with the Father. According to this theory Christ was a created being. This denial of the Trinity was condemned at Nicea in 325. [See Nicea]

Arminianism. The doctrine derived from the teachings of Jacob Arminus (1560-1609). This doctrine fundamentally teaches that man has a free will. He can either accept or reject God of his own power. Redemptive grace is universal. God does not choose anyone, but He foresees some will choose Him and on that basis God ordains them to eternal life. It is truly a salvation of works because man must do something to be saved. So it follows that man must continually save himself. This is essentially the same salvation doctrine of the semi-pelagians and the Roman Catholic Church. [Semi-Pelagianism]

Articulus Mixtus. (mixed articles) Pure articles are truths which are derived from either theology or philosophy, but mixed articles may be derived from both. The existence of God can be discovered in nature or Scripture.

Articulus stantis et cadentis ecclesiae. (the article by which the church stands or falls) This phrase was coined by Martin Luther. The article is justification by faith alone. If this is correct then any church which denies justification by faith alone ceases to be a true church. [See Justification]

Aseity. (being from itself) Refers to God's self-existence and independence. God has the power of being. He is not dependent, contingent, or derived. This word should be used regularly in Christian teaching because it recognizes a characteristic that only belongs to God, which is His independence. [See Being; Essence]

Assensus. This is part of the reformers concept of faith. It refers to the simple assent to a truth by the intellect or intellectual assent to data. It is preceded by notitia, understanding the basis of the faith, and followed by fiducia, trusting in the claims of faith. [See Faith; Notitia; Fiducia]

Athanasius. The primary defender of the orthodox view of the person and nature of Jesus Christ (*homoousios*) during the fourth century, against Arianism. He is remembered for the phrase "Anthanasius contra mundum" (Anathanasius against the world) denoting his faithfulness when most of the church was against him. [See Homoousios]

Atomistic exegesis. This refers to the mistreatment of Scripture where one is concerned with each particular word without considering the relationship of the word to the whole of Scripture. It fails to practice the analogy of faith. [See Analogy of faith]

Atonement. (the Hebrew word literally means "to cover over" or "make propitiation") The aspect of the work of Christ, particularly His death that makes possible the restoration of fellowship between God and man. The doctrine of the atonement states that Christ died and atoned for the sins of the elect. The core meaning of the atonement, for the Christian, is the satisfaction of a demand for justice. The doctrine of the atonement has been explained from several different perspectives:

1. Moral Influence Theory refers to Jesus and His self-giving love. It states that Jesus died a martyr as a victim of unjust people. This view does not reflect cosmic full satisfaction. This is a false view of the atonement according to classical Reformed theology.

2. Ransom Theory says Christ was given by God as a ransom to Satan in order to cancel the debt Satan had on man. This is a false view of the atonement according to classical Reformed theology.

3. Substitutionary Atonement teaches that the priestly work of Christ removes God's anger and wrath by the covering over of our sins through the Substitutionary sacrifice of Jesus Christ to God, thus securing acceptance for the elect. This is the view of the atonement according to orthodox Reformed theologians. [See Propitiation; Expiation]

Attributes of God. A reference to the character of God or quality of God which constitutes who He is. God's attributes are inseparable from His being. His attributes consist of his omniscience, omnipotence, omnipresence, and all the qualities that belong to God.

Aufgehoben. (overcoming) Hegel used this term in his dialectical idealism to describe the synthesis in his philosophical system. This is the upward movement to the final synthesis in the evolution process. [See Hegel; Dialectical idealism]

Augustine of Hippo. (354-430) A bishop in North Africa and held in high esteem among the Latin fathers. Western philosophers and theologians were influenced by his extensive writings. His theology was used as a standard for future western theologians to compare. [See Augustinianism]

Augustinianism. The theology of Augustine of Hippo teaches that man is morally unable to embrace the gospel because of the Fall and that the Fall is absolute and affects all that we are. The Holy Spirit monergistically (working alone) changes the heart of fallen man and enables man to understand and believe the gospel. According to Augustinianism regeneration precedes faith in the ordo salutis (order of salvation) and actually regeneration produces faith. [See Ordo slautis]

Authority. The concept of right in contradistinction to power given to the creature by the creator. The Bible says Jesus has been given "all authority in heaven and on earth" (Matthew 28:18). This means that Jesus Christ has the right to govern all of creation. God has limited the authority given to man, so that man's authority is dependent on God. [See Double truth]

Auto-piste. (trustworthy in and of itself) A term used by Protestant scholastics to denote the self-authenticating character of scriptural authority.

Autonomy. (self-law) Freedom and independent from all external constraint. The quest for autonomy is the initial sin of the human race. When God spoke through the mouth of Isaiah speaking to Babylon (I believe the text has Nebuchadnezzar in mind) the sin of autonomy comes from the mouth of the leader of Babylon "I am and there is no one besides me" (Isaiah 47:8,10).

Averroes. A 13th century Islamic philosopher who was an advocate of Integral Aristotelianism that sought a synthesis between Aristotle and Islamic theology. He proposed the doctrine of the double-truth theory, that propositions could be true in science or philosophy and false in theology, and vice-versa. The followers of Averroes took his commentaries and advanced philosophical propositions without the influence of religion. Thomas Aquinas, Bonaventure, and other 13th century theologians rejected the Latin Averroists in favor of orthodox Christianity. [See Double truth; Integral Aristotelianism]

Baptism. A sacrament of the Roman Catholic and Protestant Church. It represents cleansing from sin, a symbol of death and resurrection of Christ, regeneration, and faith. The *Westminster Confession of Faith* explains that baptism is "not only for the solemn admission of the party baptized into the visible Church; but also to be unto him a sign and seal of the covenant of grace." Many Protestant denominations reject the idea that baptism is a sacrament. [See Sacraments]

Barth, Karl. A significant theologian of the 20th century. Barth wanted to save the Bible from liberals and human philosophy. In the process he reduced the word of God to the ultimate antinomy. The result was that he would say affirming contradiction was an indication of Christian growth. He was recognized as a leader in the Neo-orthodoxy movement. [See Antinomy; Neo orthodoxy]

Beatific vision. The great hope of all believers, that in heaven they will see God as He is. Although theologians do not agree on the means to the end, this is the final destination of God's elect (Acts 7:56).

Beatitudes. (Latin, *beatitudo* which refers to blessedness) Often referred to as the Sermon of the Mount, the beatitudes are the blessings spoken by the Lord Jesus Christ to his disciples. The blessings would remind them of the nature and character of their relationship with Christ. They teach the inherent nature of Christianity and not just the morality for which they are often used.

Begotten not made. This comes from the Nicean Creed. It declares that Christ is not created, but that He exists eternally. This describes the quality of Christ as the God-man rather than an event to be celebrated. [See Nicea]

Being. The quality or state of reality often referred to as existence. Being is the explanation of reality. The study of being is applicable to philosophy and theology because "something" rather than "nothing" is the subject. [See Aseity; Essence]

Believe. (See Faith)

Benediction. (literally a "good speaking.") Refers to the words of blessing spoken by God or by his representative. Many churches use the benediction to close the formal collective worship of God's people.

Bene esse. (Good essence, well being) An essential affirmation to the well being of the faith. This term is used by some churches to refer to the well being of the church.

Biblical docetism. A term coined by Emil Brunner describing the orthodox view of inerrancy. The Docetists were a sect of Gnostics who denied Jesus had a real body. Brunner is saying that the Orthodox view of Scripture denies that men wrote it because men err. [See Docetism]

19

Big bang cosmology.   The idea that the universe exploded into being. This hypothesis is false by definition and violates the law of non-contradiction, affirming that the universe exploded before it was. [See Ex nihilo, nihil fit]

Born Again.   [See New Birth; Regeneration]

Brunner, Emil.   A noted 20th century theologian who was a student of Karl Barth.   He and Barth were associated with the neo-orthodox movement. His neo-orthodoxy was expressed in these terms: "contradiction is the hallmark of Christianity."

Bultmann's new hermeneutic.   The German theologian, Rudolf Bultmann (1884-1976), believed that the only way to bridge the historical and cultural gap, between when and where the Bible was written and the when and where we read it, the responsible interpreter must come to the text with a certain *vorverstandis*, which means a prior understanding. He did not think it was possible to discover the actual meaning of Scripture. [See Vorverstandis]

Caesarea Philippi Confession.   "Thou are the Christ, the Son of the Living God" (Matthew 16:16). Caesarea Phillipi is the location of Peter's confession of Christ as the Messiah. This is the turning point for the disciples understanding of Christ. It may be said that this is the first creed of the Christian church.

Calvin, John.   The theologian of the 16th century Reformation who wrote the first systematic theology from a Reformed perspective.   He understood and articulated the majesty and sovereignty of God more than any other theologian during his time.

Calvin's definition of free will. The ability to choose according to what you want. What you want depends on the will. The component of the soul known as the will is the factor that must be considered in light of this teaching. This is essentially the same definition as Augustine and Jonathan Edwards. [See Freedom of the will; Will]

Calvinism. The designation usually applied to the theological doctrine of John Calvin. It embodies the fundamental principle of God's sovereignty based on the analogy of faith and sola Scriptura. The doctrine of Calvin is often misunderstood since his students embraced some biblical doctrine different that Calvin himself. For instance, the Five Points of Calvinism are often assumed to come from the mind and pen of John Calvin. They were not produced until the Synod of Dort (1618) long after Calvin's death (1564). However, they do summarize the teaching of John Calvin. [See Calvin, John]

Canon. The Greek word means "rule". It is a term used to describe the recognized books of Scripture. A collection of individual inspired books contained in the Bible. There are three primary views of the canon:

1. Roman view - Infallible collection of infallible books
2. Liberal view - fallible collection of fallible books
3. Classical Reformed view - Fallible collection of infallible books.

The criteria for canonicity:
a) written or endorsed by an Apostle
b) accepted by the church
c) judging conformity of the unquestionable against the questionable

Causality.   The relationship between cause and its effect. Every effect must have a sufficient cause. It is a practical application of the law of non-contradiction. God is independent of creation thus it may be said that God is the first cause of all things. The Bible teaches that God ordained everything that has or will ever happen. His ordination included the instruments and occasions which are called second causes. For example, God the first cause ordained that the apple would fall to the ground, but He also ordained gravity which is the second cause to bring about the apple falling to the ground. [See Heisenberg principle]

Chalcedon.   Church council held in 451 A.D. to define orthodox Christology more than any previous council. The Council of Chalcedon stated that Christ is truly man and truly God without confusion, mixture, or separation. [See Chalcedonian Formulation]

Chalcedonian Formulation.   The Council of Chalcedon convened to deal with heresies relating to the deity and the humanity of Jesus Christ.   The Chalcedonian Formulation affirmed the unity of the two natures of Christ: *vere home*, (truly man) and *vere deus*, (truly God). The unity of the two natures of Christ was defined as:

1) Without mixture - directed at the Monophysite heresy

2) Without confusion - directed at the Monophysite heresy

3) Without division - directed at the Nestorian heresy

4) Without separation - directed at the Nestorian heresy

The Chalcedonian Formulation states that each nature, the human and divine, retains its own attributes. [See Monophysite; Nestorianism]

Chaos. The ancient Greeks distinguished between cosmos and chaos in that cosmos was order and sense, but chaos was disorder and nonsense. [See Cosmos]

Chiliasm. The word is derived from the Greek word that is translated "one thousand" in the Bible. This term was used in the early church, but more especially during the 16th century Reformation, to describe a theory that Christ would establish an earthly kingdom and reign for one thousand years. The mainline Reformers (Calvin at Geneva, Knox in Scotland, et al) often used this term in a pejorative sense against the radical Reformers (Anabaptists, et al.). [See Amillennialism; Premillennialism; Postmillennialism]

Christ. (Greek, *Christos* - Latin, *Christus*) It literally refers to the anointed one or the Messiah, who is anointed to the office of Mediator. Specifically a title that belongs only to the second person of the Trinity. [See Christology]

Christos victor. Christ achieves a victory over Satan and Christ is our champion.

Christology. The study of the doctrine of Christ encompassing the person and work of Christ. This is an important discipline because of the peculiar nature of Christ in His human and divine natures. [See Chalcedonian Formulation]

Church. This term is often misunderstood, misused, and misrepresented by Christians. It is derived from the Greek word *ecclesia* referring to the "the ones called out." In the early Greek city/democracy, it referred to the assembly of the citizens of a city. The Bible does not give a brief definition of the church. The building where God's people meet to fulfill the collective responsibilities is not the church. Furthermore, it is not possible to "go to church" or "meet for church" or any false notion that the church is a place, institution, or organization. Jesus Christ is the head of the church (Colossians 1:18). The church "which is His body, [is] the fullness of Him who fills all in all" (Ephesians 1:23). Therefore, the church consists of those who belong to the family of God, through the work of Christ, by the power of the Holy Spirit. The purpose of the church is worship (Psalm 95:6). The mission of the church is to make disciples and teach the full counsel of God (Matthew 28:19-20). The ministry of the church is to equip Christians to serve in the body of Christ (Ephesians 4:11-16). [See ecclesia; Ecclesiology]

Church Growth Movement. This movement uses words that are easily subject to the fallacy of equivocation in a typical discussion about the expansion of the church. The words "church growth" in a biblical sense are radically different than the words "church growth" in the context of modernity. The church growth movement can be traced to the work of Donald McGavran. He was a missionary to India, professor at Fuller Seminary and founder of the Church Growth Institute. The church growth movement has no theology, no accountability, and no set pattern for the application of the biblical concept of church expansion. The goal is to plant and develop churches using whatever tools are available with little concern for theological integrity or biblical accountability. The author of this book has written a book entitled "The god of the Church Growth Movement" in an effort to analyze the movement.

Classical Apologetics. A view that a knowledge of God and His divine attributes can be known from creation by using the classical arguments used throughout church history. It begins with self-consciousness. The classical arguments are as follows:

Cosmological - It assumes that something exists and argues from the existence of that thing to the existence of a First Cause or a sufficient reason for the creation.

Anthropological - This asks the question, how do you explain the existence of man.

Teleological - Argument to purposes or design.

Moral - Something keeps man from utter destruction. The reality of moral law requires a law-giver.

Ontological – Something exists, therefore God must exist.

The purpose of Christian apologetics:

1) Obey Scripture (1 Peter 3:15)
2) Stop the mouth of the obstreperous
3) Strengthen believers
4) Pre-evangelism value

[See Apologetics; Presuppositional apologetics]

Clement of Rome. A Bishop of Rome and one of the early church fathers. He wrote an epistle, but it was rejected in the canon, because it was recognized to be subordinate to the authority of the Apostles. However, it is a valuable work since it is one of the earliest letters after the death of the Apostles. [See Canon]

Common ground. A term used to describe the starting point for apologetics with unbelievers. All men are created in the image of God so that the laws of logic and empirical data are common to all men. [See Apologetics]

Communicable attribute.   Attributes of God for which corresponding characteristics can be found in human nature. For example, God loves, and man also loves, but not to the same degree or the same way that God loves. [Attributes of God]

Communicatio idiomata.   (communication of attributes) A term used in Christology to describe the way in which the properties of each nature are communicated in the unity of the person of Christ. Martin Luther, in his doctrine of the literal body and blood of Christ being present in the Lord's Supper, departed from the Reformed view thus believing that the human nature of Christ was made capable of omnipresence. Luther's view militates against the Chalcedonian Creed which affirms that "each nature retains its own attributes."

Compound being.   Refers to God being made up of distinct parts. The attributes of God are of His simple nature and not the pieces of a compound being. [See Simple being; Trinity; cf. Deuteronomy 6:4]

Concurrence.   This seldom used term literally means to run together with. Used in connection with the doctrine of God's providence it describes the primary and secondary causes and that they operate concurrently. God's purpose is brought to pass by his sovereignty even though he uses human means. For instance, the brothers of Joseph (Genesis 37-50) did evil, but God intended it for good. [See Providence; Causality]

Confirmation.   This is a sacrament of the Roman Catholic Church that teaches when one moves from childhood to adult new grace is given to the believer. Roman Catholic sacramental theology teaches an incremental increase of grace into its subjects beginning with baptism. [See Sacerdotalism]

Conscience. This term often used in connection with moral decisions is difficult to define from biblical language. Conscience appears to have some relation to the mind which is a metaphysical entity (See Romans 2:15; Titus 1:15). The conscience bears witness with the moral awareness of the mind. [See Mind]

Consumerism. This worldview is the manifestation of the concept known as happiness. The instant purchase of goods allegedly produces instant gratification for the consumer. This worldview also serves as a diversionary tactic to distract from the realities of life.

Contra Naturam. (works against the laws of nature) A term used to show that miracles attest the authority of Scripture. [See Causality]

Contra Peccatum. (against sin) This is the argument that only God can act against sin. It describes the limitation on Satan. [See Sin]

Contradiction. The belief that a proposition and its opposite cannot be both true at the same time and in the same relationship. Something cannot be A and -A at the same time and in the same relationship. For example, God cannot be sovereign and not sovereign at the same time and in the same relationship. [See Law of non-contradiction]

Consubstantial. This was an important word used to estab-lish the orthodox doctrine of the Trinity. It describes the hypo-static union of Jesus Christ. Hypostatic union refers to the trinity consisting of three persons in one God. It comes from the Greek word *homoousion* which literally means "of same substance." The orthodox Christian doctrine is that there is an eternal subsistence between God the Father, God the Son, and God the Holy Spirit. [See Homoousios; Hypostasis]

Cooperare and assentire. Latin words meaning "cooperate and assent." Semi-pelagians use these terms to explain that man must cooperate with and assent to prevenient grace, grace which comes before faith and regeneration, to bring about regeneration. This view teaches that faith precedes regeneration. It literally puts man in control of salvation. [See Semi-pelagianism; Arminianism; Prevenient grace; Faith; Regeneration]

Cooperative grace. [See Synergism]

Cor ecclesiae. (the heart of the church) Martin Luther said *sola fide* (faith alone), *sola scriptura* (Scripture alone), and *sola deo gloria* (the glory of God alone) was the heart of the church. [See Reformation]

Corporeal monists. Philosophers who taught that all things were made of some physical stuff such as the philosopher Thales who taught that all things were made of water. [See Thales]

Cosmological argument. This is one of several tools used by the classical apologist to prove theism. It notes the existence of the cosmos, the universe, and argues from the existence of created order to the existence of a First Cause or a sufficient reason for the creation. [See Apologetics; Classical apologetics]

Cosmology. The study of the order and harmony found in the world. Christian theology teaches that God ordered these principles, but sin prevents the perfect ordering and provokes chaos [See Chaos; Cosmological argument]

Cosmos. The name used by ancient Greeks for the universe. They were pre-occupied with order and harmony which this word describes. [See Chaos]

Council of Trent. A council of the counter reformation in 1550. They repudiated justification by faith alone, saying any who teach such should be damned. It accepted the two source theory of revelation. The two source theory accepted not only the authority of Scripture but also the traditions of the church. This council of the Roman Catholic Church is most famous for affirming justification by faith, merit, and the authority of Scripture interpreted by the church. The doctrine of justification by faith alone was rejected at this council.

Covenant of grace. This theological concept refers to the gracious operation of a covenant making God who wills to save His elect through his covenant promises. The biblical covenants that are generally accepted to constitute the covenant of grace are:

1) Adamic - Covenant of commencement
(Gen. 3:15)

2) Noahic - Covenant of preservation
(Gen. 8, 9)

3) Abrahamic - Covenant of promise
(Gen. 12, 15, 17)

4) Mosiac - Covenant of law (Ex. 6, 19, 20)

5) Davidic - Covenant of the kingdom
(2 Sam. 7)

6) New covenant - Covenant of Consummation (Jer. 31:33,34)

Covenant of works.   This was the first covenant God initiated for man to keep. This covenant involved God's promised blessing and rules for man to obey to secure God's promised blessing. This covenant of works is not without the gracious hand of God. Adam, acting as the federal head of the human race, failed to keep the covenant of works

Covenant theology.   Covenant theology describes the pattern used by Christians to define their biblical concepts and systems. It is called covenant theology because of the biblical covenant instituted by God Himself. The covenant idea expresses the relationship between God and man, but God is always the covenant maker. Man is the covenant breaker.

Covetousness.   Refers to the sin of both being dissatisfied with what God has given us, and of wishing to have that which God has given to another. One can covet material wealth, honor, family, even spiritual wealth. It also refers to wanting to have more than God's provision. [See Providence]

Creation ex nihilo.   (created out of nothing) The idea that God created without the use of previously existing materials. Everything created comes from God. God has the power of being and thus the power to create. [See Ex nihilo nihil fit]

Credo.   (I believe) The term is the first word in the Latin text of the Apostles' Creed. It describes the consciousness of a rational creature making an intelligent statement.

Credulity. In theology this refers to accepting information without much examination. It leads to easy believism. This fallacy must be rejected to maintain theological integrity. [See Exegesis; Hermeneutics]

Culture. The word culture from the Latin *cultura* refers to land and life associated with it such as tilling the soil. The related Latin word *cultus* referred to the actions and worship associated with life. The word culture refers to a way of life. For instance, a Christian culture refers to the way of life based on the teaching from the Word of God. A godly culture and a Christian stand on the same foundation.

Cutting rites. Signs and symbols of the covenant in the Old Testament. God's covenant with Abraham (Genesis. 15:17) was a cutting rite. Circumcision during the period of the Old Testament was a cutting rite signifying a covenant.

Deconstructionism. The method of interpretation used by postmodernists, denying an objective message from the author of the text. The French philosopher Jacques Derrida, is the author of deconstruction hermeneutics. This method of interpretation dismissed the validity of the Grammatical-historical method. Deconstruction demands that the text be "deconstructed" by the reader so that any internal contradictions might be removed. The intent of the author is not important, but the reader may reconstruct the text to make sense of it. [See Postmodernity]

Decretive will of God. Francis Turretin defines the decretive will of God as that "which God wills to do or permits himself." It refers to the eternal decrees of God. [See Will]

Deism. This word is derived from the Latin word *Deus* which means "God." Its Greek equivalent was the Greek word *theos* for God. The words *deus*, (Latin for God), *theos*, (Greek for God) and God (English for God) have different meanings according to cultures and religions at different times in history. Since word meanings change over the course of time it is important to interpret language in light of its objectivity, orthodoxy and the logic of the language. The word deism took on a different meaning during the 17th century in the western world. During that period of time several theologians and philosophers described themselves as deists. They believed that God was the supreme and sovereign Creator, but that God created the world with laws that would sustain and regulate the orderliness of creation. This left the operation of God's providence to the laws of nature. The result was the denial of God's immanence while maintaining the belief in the transcendence of God. [See Immanence; Theism; Transcendence]

Descartes, Rene. A French philosopher of the 17th century who sought to explain the relation and interaction between matter and thought. He sought to understand the relation between extension and non-extension. Descartes described matter as extension and thought as non-extension. He coined the Latin phrase *Cogito ergo sum*, "I think therefore, I am."

De servo abritrium. (concerning bound choice) Luther's Latin expression of the bondage of the will, which affirms that the will of the unregenerate can only sin and thus cannot come to faith of its own. The enslaved will chooses according to its nature. This term was borrowed from the work of St. Augustine. [See Will]

Despotes. (Greek word meaning lord or master). It means absolute authority to legislate. This word refers to a despot. In this sinful world a despot is often tyrannical and oppressive because he usurps authority. The reference in Jude verse four to "our Lord" comes from the Greek word *despotas*. Therefore the Bible uses the word despot in a positive reference to God. God's authority is not tyrannical or oppressive, but it does include His legislative capacity as well as authority to act on legislation.

Determinism. Human choices are determined by outside forces or causes which are blind impersonal forces. We have no choice. This was John L. Girardeau's charge against Jonathan Edwards and his work on the Freedom of the Will. Those who argue for determinism are said to establish fatalism and therefore a rejection of personal responsibility especially in the realm of ethics. Those who argue against determinism are said to denigrate the sovereignty of God. Christians must closely examine the Biblical doctrine of predestination and free will in relation to this highly controversial word. [See Will]

Deus absconditus. (that which God has not revealed to us). A phrase used by Luther to describe the knowledge of God which remains a mystery to man because God has chosen not to reveal certain information about Himself. [See Mystery]

Deus revelatus. (God's revelation) A phrase used by Luther to describe the knowledge of God which is revealed especially in the incarnation of Jesus Christ, the second person of the Trinity. [See Revelation]

Dialectic. This comes from the word dialogue which means back and forth. Hegel, the German Idealist philosopher developed Dialectical Idealism. The dialectic is a tension, struggle, and conflict. All knowledge begins with a thesis, then to a proposition, on to the anti-thesis, the opposite of the thesis, and the final step in this evolutionary process is the synthesis which becomes a new thesis. [See Dialectical idealism]

Dialectical Idealism. Hegel's philosophy in a three stage operation.
1) Thesis;
2) Antithesis;
3) Synthesis.

This a process to understand the progression and movement of history. The philosophical systems emerging from Hegel have produced world views contrary to Scripture because those systems seek to discover the nature of reality. [See Hegel]

Dialectical Materialism. Marx's philosophy which stated that the conflict in history is not over ideas, but over material goods and the means of production. [See Marx, Karl]

Diderot. French philosopher of the Enlightenment. He said the God hypothesis was no longer necessary to explain the origin of the universe and of life. He argued for spontaneous generation.

Dignitas. (dignity) A word closely connected to the Latin word *gloria*, thus the glory of God is the dignity of God. The human response is to give God what He is due which is worship above all things. [See Gloria; Gravitas]

Dispensation. In Christian theology this refers to the ordering of God's economy. It is the sequence of events that occur in the history of redemption.

Dispensational theology. This relatively recent (roughly 150 years old) system of theology essentially divides Scripture into a number of different "economies", or of different ways in which God deals with the history of man and redemption. The following are common distinctives of this view:

1) The denial of the moral necessity of obeying the law of God;
2) The sharp division between the Old and New Testament;

3) The disbelief in the current reign of Christ, and the spread of the kingdom over the earth before His return. As with any theological system it is diverse and many views emerge from it.

Docetism. The heretical view that the body of Christ was not real, but only seemed or appeared to be real. The Gnostics in the early Church were docetists because they denied the real humanity and the real suffering of Christ. [See Biblical docetism]

Documentary hypothesis theory. (JEDP interpretation of Scripture). The Graff-Wellhausen hypothesis seems to suggest that a dynamic revelation is applied to Scripture. It suggests that four different authors penned the Pentateuch. The authorship of the Pentateuch, according to this hypothesis is:

1) Jehovist – His contribution to the Pentateuch was of the Davidic period of the Old Testament.

2) Elohist – A writer from the northern kingodm emphasizing the northern tribes.

3) Deuteronomists – He wrote primarily Deuternomy in support of Josiah's reforms.

4) Priestly writers – These were primarily responsible for the redaction and compilation of the Pentateuch during or after the exile.

This essentially denies plenary (full, complete) verbal inspiration of Scripture. It naturally follows that dynamic revelation popularized by the neo-orthodox scholars taught that the Bible becomes the Word of God through some kind of encounter with Scripture. [See Plenary verbal inspiration]

Double predestination. This is a misnomer often used in theological discussion. Arminians and anti-Calvinists use this term to teach that God chooses some to be saved and chooses some to be lost. Every person makes a decision to accept Christ or deny Christ based on the condition of the will (soul). The Bible gives an accurate description of what happens when the will has been changed. "And a certain woman named Lydia, from the city of Thyatira, a seller of purple fabrics, a worshiper of God, was listening; and the Lord opened her heart to respond to the things spoken by Paul" (Acts 16:14). It was not the gospel message that changed the heart of Lydia because the Bible says "the Lord opened her heart." Before the Lord opened her heart, she had a closed heart. The action, represented by the word opened, is something that happened to her. Predestination is an act of God whereby he ordains whatsoever comes to pass. The church would do well to leave this mystery into the hands of a sovereign God and pursue the mission and ministry without controversy. [See Predestination]

Double Truth. Theory propagated by Islamic philosophers of the 12th and 13th century that taught something could be true in reason and false in faith and vice versa. It indicates a divorce between nature and grace. [See Averroes; Integral Aristotelianism]

Dualism. Two substances or powers, neither of which is reducible to the other. In Christian theology this philosophical world view denies the aseity of God. [See Aseity]

Dynamic equivalency. A form of Biblical translation which conveys thought for thought instead of word for word. The New International Version (NIV) uses this translation concept.

Dynamic monarchism. The declaration that the human

Jesus was deified (made to be God) by the divine Logos from Baptism to crucifixion and adopted by the Father after Jesus died. This trinitarian heresy was clarified by the Council of Chalcedon. [See Chalcedonian formulation]

Ebed Yahweh.   The Servant of the Lord (Isaiah 42:19) is the one punished as the Sin-bearer. This was not popular among the Jewish people because they could not imagine a humiliated, suffering and slain Messiah. They did not want the slain lamb, they wanted the Lion of Judah.

Ecce homo.   (behold the man) A common expression used by theological liberals in the 19th century to focus on the historical Jesus rather than the metaphysical Jesus, referring back to the declaration of Pilate regarding Jesus.

Ecclesia.   The Greek term referring to the "called assembly." Christianity uses it to describe the church because the Bible uses the term to define the church. [See Ecclesiology; Church]

Ecclesiology.   This important term derived from the Greek work *ecclesia* is often translated church. It is a theological discipline focusing on the nature, purpose, mission, and ministry of the church. [See Ecclesia; Church]

Edwards, Jonathan.   Often referred to as America's greatest thinker, Edwards was a pastor, theologian, philosopher, and metaphysician. He is thought to be the last great Puritan. He was reformed in his world and life view, Calvinistic in his doctrine, Covenantal in his theology, and a classical apologist par excellent. Jonathan Edwards taught boldly on the concept "why men hate God." Edwards said it is because God is holy, omnipotent, omniscient, and immutable. Man knows God's power will never decrease so man loses the spark of divinity.

Efficacy. A word used in theological discourse to describe that which actually produces the desired result.

Effectual calling. A term used to describe that part of the ordo salutis (order of salvation) that is first in the order of our limited understanding of the application of God's grace. It is a calling that brings about the desired effect, thus it is efficacious. Those who are effectually called actually come to faith. [See Ordo salutis]

Emotions. The aspect of the soul that communicates the decision of the will and of the thinking mind. Another word used to describe human emotions is affections. Jonathan Edwards wrote a book entitled *Religious Affections.* He "argues that while affections are the heart of religion, they nevertheless must begin in the mind" (Rational Biblical Theology of Jonathan Edwards, vol. 3, p. 288). Emotional responses or affections are expressed by love, fear, grief, joy, and many more similar words. [See Mind; Soul; Will]

Empiricism. A philosophical view that teaches the source of all knowledge is sense experience. It is based on the common perception that our senses provide us with truth. As a world and life view the logical end of empiricism is that experience is the sole source of knowledge. Empiricism stands in stark contrast to Rationalism. [See Rationalism]

Enlightenment. The philosophy of European rationalists during the 18th century. It rejected supernatural revelation and man's sinfulness, but crowned reason as its god. It likewise suggested that men and society are perfectible using the proper use of reason. The continental Enlightenment gave life to deism in England and America. [See Deism]

Ens necessarium. (necessary being) According to Aquinas, God is the necessary being, or cause for all else to be. [See Being; Essence]

Envy. The sin of being dissatisfied with the providence of God, brought forth by loving the thing desired inordinately, that is, out of proportion.

Epistemology. The science or study of knowledge. It answers the question: How do we know what we know? The theory of knowledge is essential for theological inquiry. The quest for truth cannot be separated from a knowledge of God. Non-negotiables for knowledge:

1) Law of non-contradiction
2) Law of causality
3) Basic reliability of sense perception
4) The ability of words to communicate
5) Applying the laws of logic to language
[See Logic]

Equal ultimacy. A view of God's decrees where God is creating good. This teaches that God ordained evil, but does not do evil. This is another controversial issue that is best left to the mystery of God's plan.

Eschatology. A branch of theology concerned with the study of final things in the Christian church, especially the second coming of Christ, the resurrection, the final judgment, and eternal consequences. The discussions of millennial views are often a major consideration for this theological discipline. [See Amillennialism; Premillennialism; Postmillennialism]

Esse. (to be; essence) This describes that which is essential to the faith. For example justification by faith is essential to the faith.

Essence. (from the Greek word *ousia* which means being) The being or power of a thing; from the Latin *esse*, "to be." In the ancient world essence was pure being, therefore God is pure being. Although many scholars equate essence and existence, there are those who insist that essence must be distinguished from existence. [See Being; Existence; Existere; Existentialism]

Eutyches. A fourth century heretic who fused two natures in one person (half man, half God) and so emphasizes the deity of Christ his humanity was neglected. He was condemned at Chalcedon in 451 and deposed from his office. [See Chalcedonian Formulation]

Evidentialist. Relative to Christian apologetics this refers to one who presents valid evidence that man is morally obligated to God. This view of apologetics often called a probalist has been charged with only proving the probability that God exists. There is a difference between an evidentialist and a classical apologist. [See Classical Apologetics]

Evil. The negation of good. It is wicked, real, and experienced, and that which is morally bad or harmful.

Evolutionary theory of the 19th century. The theory in which the doctrine of evolution played major roles in disciplines such as sociology and psychology. It was also a factor in political theory, the scientific world and Christian theology.

Exaltation of Christ. A reference to the resurrection of Christ, His ascension into heaven, sitting at the right hand of God the Father, and in coming to judge the world at the last day.

Exegesis.   (from a Greek word meaning to search out or literally draw out of). It refers to using the proper tools and instruments to discover and understand the true meaning of any biblical text. Therefore, the Bible is interpreted and explained. The meaning of the biblical text, which is one meaning, is then applied to any given situation. The pastor must know and practice sound exegesis to properly equipment his congregation for works of service. [See Hermeneutics]

Ex lex controversy.   In the middle ages it was the tension between the internal righteousness of God and the external righteousness of God. (i.e.-What is the relationship of God and the law?) Is God bound by the law, or is He above the law? God is the morally perfect law maker therefore God cannot break the law nor can He make a law higher than Himself.

Ex nihilo.   (out of nothing) This term allegedly defines how the world was created out of nothing or without any pre-existing matter.   Christian theology acknowledges that creation was without any pre-existing matter.   There is no possibility of something coming from nothing. [See Ex nihilo nihil fit]

Ex nihilo nihil fit.   (out of nothing, nothing comes) Self explanatory.

Ex opere operato.   (by the work performed) The belief that when the sacraments are administered they are effective to act positively upon the believer or unbeliever according to the Roman Catholic Church.   For instance, the act of baptism actually justifies the recipient. Also known as sacerdotalism. [See Sacerdotalism]

Existence.   This comes from a Latin term meaning to stand out of. The ancient Greeks would say this is becoming. It refers to the realm of creaturely being, not in the realm of being or what some philosophers call "isness". [See essence; existere]

Existentialism. A philosophy which begins with the idea that existence precedes essence and that we decide what we are, and what everything else is.

Existere. (to stand out of) Could be referred to as a state of becoming. The realm of creaturely being (in the sense that the created world stands out of pure being, because it is changing or becoming), but also is used to refer to the being of God (in the sense that He stands out of the creation). [See Existence]

Exousia. Greek word meaning authority or right. It comes from the Greek preposition *ex* which means out of and *ousia* which means being or essence. The Bible says Jesus had authority to teach, to forgive sins, et. al. because He is the source of all being. God gives His creatures authority, but it is limited and temporal.

Expiation. This a work of Christ directed to man for removal of guilt. Christ removes the penalty of sin from us. [See propitiation]

Extreme unction. A Roman Catholic sacrament to relieve mortal sin before death. [See Mortal sin]

Fabricum idolarum. (an idol factory) John Calvin used this term and taught that "everyone of us, even from his mother's womb, is expert in inventing idols" (*Calvin's Commentary on the Book of Acts*, Vol. 19, p. 413).

Faith. To believe, and in the context of Christian theology, to believe God. Saving faith has historically been understood to consist of three constituent parts.

1) notitia, which is the grasping of the concepts inherent in saving faith.

2) assensus, which is the affirmation that these concepts are true.

3) fiducia to trust in those concepts.

These distinctions are critical, for the devil himself understands the gospel, and knows that it is true, yet hates it. Note that this understanding says nothing of believing despite, contrary or in the absence of evidence. Biblical faith is not a leap in the dark, or something to be contrasted with knowledge, but a conscious trust in truths that can be demonstrated. [See Credo; Assensus; Fiducia; Notitia]

Fallible collection of fallible books. A modern liberal theory which describes the canon of Scripture. This view is the full and final rejection of the authority of Scripture. [See Sola scriptura]

Fallible collection of infallible books. The Classical Christian view of the canon of Scripture. The intent is to state that the church received the books and the church is fallible. The inspired word of God is infallible. Therefore the church as a fallible institution has collected canon of Scripture which consists of infallible books. [See Canon]

Federal headship. [See Federal theology]

Federal theology. Adam, the perfect representative for the human race, was chosen by a sovereign, omnipotent, omniscient, and holy God to be the federal head of the human race. It is representation by imputation. Adam failed in his covenant responsibilities so that all men sinned in Adam's sin and his sin is imputed to all men. It was not Adam's particular sin, but the guilt of Adam's sin nature that was imputed. Jesus Christ is the second Adam in which the elect are redeemed. He fulfilled all God's covenant promises. [Covenant theology]

Feurbach.   Philosopher who stated that man created God in man's image. Gods are mirror images of the people that worship them. For instance, Oriental gods had slanted eyes, the god of the white man is white, et al. Marx came under the influence of Feurbach's atheism. [See Marx, Karl]

Fideism.   (The Latin word *fide* literally means faith and the English "ism" is a noun forming suffix often associated with a world view). It means to believe something by faith without any rational evidence. There is an old maxim attributed to St. Hilary of the 5th century that says "A person cannot express what he does not know and he cannot believe what he cannot express." Fideism will produce theological disaster because it has no metaphysical basis.

Fides historica.   (historical faith) This is the mere acceptance of data as true apart from any spiritual effect. [See Assensus; Faith]

Fides implicitum.   (implicit faith) The Roman Catholic Church required the Christian to give complete submission to the interpretation of the church by faith. It was reaffirmed at the 4th session of the Council of Trent.

Fides salvifica.   (saving faith) This faith accepts the promises of God to the salvation of the soul.

Fides viva.   (living faith) This is associated with the Reformers view of justification by faith alone. It suggests, with the book of James, that true faith is necessarily a living faith, which yields good works.

Fiducia. This refers to trust. It fits in the reformers view of faith to include *notitia* (knowledge) and *assensus* (to affirm or to agree). [See Faith; Assensus; Notitia]

Filioque. This Latin word means "and the son." This phrase was added to the Nicene Creed indicating that the Holy Spirit proceeded from the Father and Son, which led to a division between the Eastern Church and the Western Church. The controversy is trinitarian in nature. The biblical text used by both sides is John 15:26.

Finite. This term used in theology refers to the dependent creation, especially dependent rational creatures. Man is dependent in comparison to God who is absolutely independent. [See Infinite]

Finitum non capax infinitum. (the finite is incapable of grasping or containing the infinite). Man (finite) cannot totally comprehend God who is infinite. John Calvin used this Latin phrase to describe the immanence and transcendence of God to sinful men. [See Immanence; Transcendent]

Forensic justification. The Protestant position that justification is a legal declaration of God. Man is formally and judicially reckoned to be righteous based on the righteousness of Christ, received by faith alone. [See Analytical justification; Justification; Legal fiction]

Forgiveness. Biblical forgiveness is to have one's sins covered or remembered no more. When God forgives naturally

He still "remembers" our sin in the sense that He is omniscient and knows all things. But God no longer holds those sins against us and grants us peace. That forgiveness though free to us comes only through the atoning work of Christ and is applied only to those who trust in that work alone. Having been fully forgiven by God, the Christian is called to forgive others who sin against him or her.

Free will. A term used to describe man's inclination. Jonathan Edwards wrote an entire book entitled *Freedom of the Will* in which he said, "an act of the will is the same as an act of choosing or choice." Man is bound to his inclination often misunderstood as autonomy. [See Autonomy]

Freud's theory of the origin of religion. He said religion was invented to fill psychological felt needs. (i.e. - man has a built in fear of nature and needs to personalize the impersonal forces).

Futurist. A broad term used to describe all those who see the great bulk of New Testament eschatological prophecy to be yet in the future. [See Eschatology; Historicist; Preterist]

General revelation. God reveals Himself and some His divine attributes (power, presence, etc) to all men that is also general, or less specific in content such as saving truth, trinity, etc. [See Revelation]

Gloria. The Latin word for glory. It refers to the glory of God and is closely related to the Latin *dignitas* meaning dignity and thus the glory of God is the dignity of God. The word glory comes from the Hebrew word *kabod*, which may also be translated honor or splendor. Any reference to God is the highest form of dignity, glory, and honor. [See Dignitis; Gravitas]

Gnosticism. A religious movement that stressed salvation through knowledge. They were concerned as to how to obtain knowledge. Gnosticism rejects the idea that truth could be obtained through reason or sense perception.

Good. The English dictionary gives fifty nuances to the definition of good. Theologians strive to make distinctions relative to good(ness). There are levels of good in relation to activity and becoming. However, the essence of good belongs to God alone. [See Summum Bonum]

Good works. The theological formulation known as "good works" is often misunderstood. The best definition to my knowledge was given by Dr. John Gerstner and I will use his paradigm. He defined works in these terms:

1. Good Good - Dr. John Gerstner's expression of good works coming from a regenerate heart. This category of good works is good for the believer. Furthermore the actions and motives in doing good works were good.

2. Good Evil - Dr. John Gerstner's expression of good works coming from a regenerate heart. This category of good works is good for the believer but the actions and motives in doing it were evil.

3. Evil Good – Dr. John Gerstner's expression of good works coming from an unregenerate heart. Although the works may be good, they are bad for the unbeliever because his heart is hardened, but the motives and actions were good. God still carries out His plan even through the unbeliever.

4. Evil Evil – Dr. John Gerstner's expression of evil works. These works are evil in and of themselves and they are bad for the unbeliever because he is hardened and the motives and the

actions in doing the deed were evil. However, it is good because God's plan is accomplished.

Government. God governs the world by his absolute authority and power. He has the right and ability to govern all things that come to pass. [See Providence]

Grammatico-historical exegesis. The hermeneutical (method of interpretation) method used to determine the intended meaning of words in Scripture. The question must be asked: what did the writer intend to say? Words in Scripture are to be taken literally unless they are obviously figurative. The history (context) of Scripture must be considered in biblical interpretation. The goal is an objective understanding of the Word of God. [See Analogy of faith; Hermeneutics]

Gravitas. The Latin word for importance, esteem and majesty. The English word gravity comes from this and relates to the glory of God. [See Dignitas; Gloria]

Hegel, G. W .F. An influential German philosopher of the 19th century. His philosophy was called Dialectical Idealism which is a three stage operation:

1) thesis;
2) antithesis;
3) synthesis.

His philosophy has produced a watershed effect particularly attractive to liberal Christian theology. [See Dialectical idealism]

Heisenberg principle. The term is relative to physics, but had a significant part in changing the thinking of some Christian theologians and their watershed effect. It states that we cannot

determine what causes the pattern of motion in subatomic particles. Following this principle is quantum physics which states
that a sub atomic particle can move from one point to another
without traversing the space in between. If the cause cannot be
determined then it leads to the assumption that there is no cause.
It is then assumed by some people that God was not the "necessary" or "sufficient" cause for creation. [See Causality; Indeterminacy theory; Laws regulating intelligent human discourse;]

Henotheism. The Greek words *henos* and *theos* combined,
refers to "one god." The historical critical school believed
everything moved from the simple to the complex. Therefore,
they argue this is the transitional form between polythesim and
monotheism, wherein each culture had one god. [See Monotheism; Pantheism]

Heraclitus. A pre-Socratic Greek philosopher who believed
everything was constantly changing or in the process of becoming. He said "Whatever is, is becoming." Although change in
this physical world is inevitable, everything including God is not
changing. God's nature and character is incapable of change.

Heresy. John Calvin interprets St. Augustine's understanding
of heresy by describing a heretic: "heretics corrupt the sincerity
of the faith with false dogmas" (*Institutes of the Christian
Religion,* Book IV, Chapter II, Section 5). Although Augustine's
understanding of heresy may be accepted by the majority of the
Christian church it is not enough to charge someone with heresy,
but it must be proven by the accepted rules of interpretation
applied to the word of God. The Roman Catholic Church says
the Protestant church has followed the way of heresy. Martin
Luther was excommunicated because of heresy. The Protestant
church on the other hand says the Roman Catholic church is
heretical. The word heresy most often refers to the presence of
doctrinal error in relation to the orthodox or the rules of faith

accepted by the church. Heresy in the church can be largely corrected by confessional statements that summarize the teaching of the whole counsel of God. The sad commentary is that many local churches despise confessional statements. [See Orthodoxy]

Hermeneutics. When applied to the Christian religion, this word refers to the science of biblical interpretation. It deals with rules of exegesis and its purpose is to understand the intended meaning of a communication, especially the Bible. [See Exegesis]

Historical critical school. They claimed that religion follows a definite historical pattern moving from animism to polytheism to henotheism and finally to monotheism. Philosophically it views everything moving from the simple to the complex. [See Documentary hypothesis theory]

Historicist. A broad term used to describe all those who see the bulk or all of New Testament eschatological prophecy to have happened already, usually in the events surrounding the destruction of Jerusalem and the Temple in 70 AD. Those who hold that there are still prophecies to be fulfilled, such as the resurrection of the dead, are often labeled partial or modified preterists. Those who hold to the doctrine that all prophecy has been fulfilled are often called full or hyper-preterists. [See Eschatology; Futurist; Preterist]

History. The Greek word *historeo* refers to inquiry. The most common definition is an inquiry into the past. Biblical history is different because the only inspired history is the Bible. Biblical history is descriptive history or normative history. Descriptive history describes something that happened, but militates against normative history. David's sin against Bethsheba was descriptive, but not normative. Normative history describes something that is normal for the Christian within the biblical/historical context. The Ten Commandments describe normative history. The present crisis in the church is a result of the ignorance of historical truth and rebellion against the God of history. The lack of interest in the philosophy of history is the primary contributing factor. As George Hegel claimed the history of philosophy is, "the thoughtful consideration of it" [history]. The first thoughtful consideration is the inspired history of Holy Scripture. The second thoughtful consideration is the use of intelligent laws of discourse to interpret secular history.

Hoc est corpus meun.   (This is my body; Matthew 26:26). These were the famous words used by Martin Luther to describe his literal approach to the sacrament of the Lord's Supper. When Jesus said, "This is my body" Luther took a literal understanding of the phrase (Matthew 26:26). Essentially that phrase was the dividing factor between the other Reformers and Luther. [See Analogy of faith; Exegesis; Hermeneutics]

Holy.   (From the Hebrew word *qodesh* meaning apartness or sacredness). The primary idea is holiness which includes God's moral perfection, but also His unique status as the sole Creator, the only being that is self-existent, eternal, infinite, etc. God may and does set apart people, places and things as holy, consecrated for His use and glory.

Homologoumena.   (Greek word meaning to agree or to allow). These are the New Testament books of the Bible accepted by the church throughout the ages.

Homo mensura.   (man the measure) A term coined by a Greek Philosopher Protagoras which means man is the measure of all things. This view expects anything real and observable to be relative to man's existence. This term is the battle cry of the humanist. [See Protagoras; Humanism]

Homo religious. (man the religious) A term coined by 19th century apologists. The question was, if God is dead why are so many people religious? They found people had a passion for religion. [See Natural theology and General revelation]

Homoousios. A Greek term meaning "the same substance." The Nicene Council affirmed that Jesus Christ is of the same essence or substance as God the Father. This was the doctrine of St. Athanasius and orthodox Christianity. It may be said that a simple Greek diphthong separates true Christology from false Christology.   [See Chalcedonian formulation; Christology; Homoiousios]

Homoiousios.   A   Greek term meaning "like substance." This is the term used to describe the Arian view of the Trinity. This word makes Jesus Christ, the second person of the Trinity, subordinate to God the Father. [See Chalcedonian formulation; Christology; Homoousios]

Humanism.   This worldview teaches that man is the highest order of being and that there is no standard above man to provide truth or morality. Though this doctrine began in the garden of Eden with the promise to Adam and Eve that they would be as God, and though it was held by the Greek philosopher Protagoras, this doctrine rose to greatest prominence in the west with the 17th century Enlightenment. This term is often used with the word secularism, because both terms see no reality beyond secular life. [See Homo mensura; Protagoras; Secularism]

Humanum errare est.   (to err is human) Used in connection with Biblical docetism. (i.e.- Jesus was human, so Jesus could err according to Karl Barth). [See Biblical docetism; Docetism]

Hume, David. This 18th century Scottish philosopher is noted for his skepticism. His attack against the law of causality did not destroy causality (every effect must have a sufficient cause), but he did question the validity of causality.

Humiliation of Christ. The low condition of Jesus Christ beginning with His incarnation, life, and death. His state of humiliation is best described by the *kenosis* passage in Philippians 2:7. [See Kenosis]

Hypocrite. One who pretends to be something he is not, particularly as it relates to morality. A hypocrite not only condemns sin of which he is guilty, but does so while claiming not to be guilty of the sin. While some complain that the church is full of hypocrites, and while such a view has some merit, it should be remembered that admission into the church requires a public confession of one's sinfulness.

Hypostasis. This Greek word may be translated "subsistence" or "reality". Thus it refers to substance, nature, or essence (*Greek Lexicon Abridged*, by Liddell and Scott). The Biblical doctrine associated with the use of the word hypostasis is the hypostatic union. It describes the unique relationship of the divine nature and the human nature of Jesus Christ joined together into one person forever. [See Trinity]

Idea of the Holy. A book written by the German Scholar Rudolph Otto who best defined the cultural sense of the holy. This book explores the mystery, transcendence, and holiness of God from a creaturely perspective. [See Otto, Rudolph; *Mysterium tremendum*]

Illumination. The process by which God's Holy Spirit enables us to understand His word and apply it to our lives. The internal working of the Holy Spirit gives the hearer or reader of the Bible, understanding to comprehend its meaning, so that there is a conviction of certainty of its divine origin and its truth.

Imago Dei. (in the likeness of God) In Christian theology this term generally refers to the qualities present in human beings that reflect, in some sense, aspects of God's nature and character. John Calvin's explanation for the *imago dei* was "there is no doubt that the proper seat of his image is in the soul" (*Institutes of the Christian Religion*, Book 1, Chapter 15, Section 3). Man's likeness to God is not in physical appearance, but rather in the soul. Man has a rational mind, so does God. Man has affections, so does God. Man has a will, so does God. However, the mind, the affections, and the will were so affected by the Fall that the mind often functions as an irrational faculty of the soul. Man's affections are often irreverent and his will is capricious. The full essence of God's revelation of Himself is in Jesus Christ, the essential *imago dei* (Colossians 2:9-10). [See Analogia entis]

Immanence. This doctrine must be seen in light of God's transcendent nature, that is, He stands above the created order. However his omnipresence (everywhere present at one time) gives Christians the assurance that God is not aloof, distant, or disinterested in His creation (as deists hold). Rather God's immanence holds that God is actively involved in this world, and in our own lives. [See Transcendence; Omnipresence]

Immediate general revelation. Revelation comes directly from God to us. Everybody has a sense of the divine. This is the certain knowledge of God which man can know by innate sense which God puts in the mind of man. This is God's self-disclosure without any medium. The "law written in their hearts" is a biblical argument for the innate knowledge of God (Romans 2:15ff) expressed in terms of immediate general revelation. [See General revelation; *Sensus divinatatus*]

Immensity of God. Teaches that God is not only ubiquitous (present everywhere), but is in His fullness everywhere. It represents the fullness of God's nature and character. [See Omnipresence]

Immutability. (unable to change) Relative to Christian theology this refers to God's unchanging character. Specifically God's character and personality does not change.

Imputation of grace. Christ's righteousness is imputed or credited to the account of the sinner and the sinner's sin is credited to Christ so that it is a real transfer.

Imprecatory Psalms. (A few examples - Psalm 35:19-26; 68:1,2; 137:8,9) Those Psalms which most clearly call upon God's judgment to prevail over His enemies. The church has not only argued over whether we can pray such prayers, but has struggled with how to understand these in the context of the grace of God, and his command that we love our enemies. These difficulties are greatly alleviated if we understand these words as coming from the mouth of Christ, who in His innocence, can and does judge the guilty. In Him, and for His glory we may likewise pray them.

Incommunicable attribute. Something God has that He does not give to His creatures. There is no corresponding characteristic found in human nature, such as immutability, simplicity, and infallibility.

Incomprehensibility of God. The first doctrine of Reformed Theology. It is not possible to understand God totally, because we are finite and He is infinite. We are not only limited, but God has limited what may be known of Him in His Special Revelation. [See *Finitum non capax infinitum*]

Incorporeal monists. Philosophers who looked for something metaphysical to be the unifying factor of all things.

Indeterminacy theory. In physics it states that sub atomic particles are unpredictable. We can predict where or when, but not both. [See Heisenberg principle]

Indicia. (indicate) The objective proof that the Bible is the Word of God. Calvin believed they were indicators for the evidence of the Bible's inspiration.

Individualism. This worldview places priority on the power of the individual creature instead of the sovereign God. Christians are the only people who are really and eternally given individual rights and at the same time Christians are under the rule of a sovereign monarch, the Lord Jesus Christ. Jesus said, "You shall know the truth, and the truth shall make you free" (John 8:32). A Christian is one who is adopted into the family of God and is an individual sibling among many siblings. It is the duty of all Christians to reject the philosophy of individualism and accept the sovereignty of God as the ruling principle in life.

Individuation. This involves discriminating one thing from other things by noting its peculiar characteristics, both similarities and differences. [See Taxonomy]

Indulgences. The doctrine of the Roman Catholic Church closely associated with the sacrament of Penance. An indulgence insures the purchase of remission of sin for temporal punishment for either the living or the dead. It essentially transfers surplus merit from the treasury of merit to a person deficient in merit.

Inerrant. A term which means that the Bible is without error in the original manuscripts. The doctrine of biblical inerrancy has been abused by fundamentalism and liberalism but in different ways. [See Inspiration]

Infallible. [See infallibility]

Infallible collection of infallible books. The Roman Catholic view of the canon of Scripture. The church claims it has infallibly collected the canon.

Infallible rule of faith and practice. This terminology was used in neo-orthodoxy to explain that the Bible is only infallible when it speaks of matters of faith and practice.

Infallibility. A term which means "the Scriptures cannot err." It refers to the full trustworthiness of the Bible so that the Bible is not deceived nor does it deceive.

Infinite. In theology this term refers to God and all His divine boundless attributes. His infinite nature extends beyond full human comprehension. [See Finite; *Finitum non capax infinitum*]

Informal fallacy. The wrong use of words and English grammar which invalidate an argument.

Infusion of Grace. The Roman Catholic Church teaches that the soul is filled with grace through baptism.
The infusion of grace is the basis of regeneration.

Infralapsarianism. (From *infra* meaning "below" and *lapsus* meaning fall) This term is often used in conjunction with the doctrine of predestination. God created Adam righteous, but Adam had the ability to sin. It holds that God's decrees of election came, logically, after the fall. [See Supralapsarianism]

Inspiration. God in His full power used men and their full power for the writing of Scripture. God superintended the work by His power and protection so that the final results in the original manuscripts were with out error. [See Inerrant]

Instrumental cause of justification per Reformers. The Protestant Church teaches that faith is the alone instrument by which the elect are justified.

Instrumental cause of justification per Rome. The Roman Catholic Church teaches that baptism and penance are the instruments of justification. Baptism is a one time sacrament whereby justifying grace is infused into the soul. However, that grace can be lost by committing a mortal sin. The Sacrament of penance is then the instrument by which justifying grace may be obtained again which is called the second plank of justification.

Integral Aristotelianism. A term that describes the Islamic philosophers of the 13th century as proposers of the of the double truth theory that something could be true in reason and false in faith or vice versa. [See Averroes; Double truth]

Interactionism. The philosopher, Rene Descartes, used this term to explain the relation and interaction between matter (extension) and thought (nonextension). [See Descartes]

Internal Testimony of Holy Spirit. Calvin used this term to describe the testimony of God's Spirit through His Word which convicts the world of sin, righteousness, and judgment.

Irresistible grace. (sometimes referred to as effectual grace) God's grace cannot be resisted when God desires the application of His grace.

Jehovah Jireh.   From the Hebrew text it means the "Lord who provides". Used in Genesis 22, the Lord provides a ram as a substitututionary sacrifice in the place of Issac. Ultimately the Lord provides a substitutionary sacrifice to atone for the sins of God's elect.

Joy.   A gift from God that brings delight and pleasure to the soul reflected by God's favorable relation to the sinner. Peace refers to a favorable relationship with God, so the Bible says, "counselors of peace have joy" (Proverbs 12:20). The character of joy does not diminish or increase relative to circumstances such as suffering and tribulation.

Judgment.   [See Krisis]

Justice.   Righteousness and justice are often used in the Bible to signify the same concept.   The justice of God is the righteousness of God demonstrated by His perfect judgment. Theologians distinguish between God distributive justice (rewards for keeping God's commandments) and retributive justice (wrath for disobeying God's commandments).   God demands justice in human affairs (Micah 6:8; Matthew 23:23).

Justification.   An act of God so that God *declares* the believer righteous. God judges the believer to be innocent based on the imputed righteousness of Christ. Justification is found in the Old Testament (See Genesis 15:6) and the New Testament (See Romans 5:1). [See Instrumental cause of justification per Reformers; Instrumental cause of justification per Rome]

Justitia alienum.   (an alien righteousness) The Protestant view of justification teaches that Christ declares one righteous. *Justitia alienum* is the charge of the Roman Catholic Church against the Reformers.   Rome called the Reformers view of justification by faith alone "alien" because under analysis the professing believer was not made righteous. According to Rome the righteousness professed by the Protestant was alien to the believer. [See Analytical justification; Forensic justification; Justification; Legal fiction]

Justitia internum. (the internal righteousness of God) This refers to God's intrinsic character. Theologians must distinguish between the internal righteousness of God and the external.

Justitia externum. The external righteousness of God referring to His goodness. It describes God's behavior and activity in the created universe. Theologians must distinguish between the internal righteousness of God and the external.

Kabod. The Hebrew word translated honor, glory, or splendor. The root of the word refers to weightiness or heaviness, thus referring to the substance and stature of God. [See *Dignitas*; Gloria; *Gravitas*]

Kant, Immanuel. (1724-1804) This German philosopher constructed an argument against rationalism. His resulting theories of knowledge and causality denied the classical use of reason and postulated a moral argument for the existence of God. [See Noumenal world; Phenomenal world]

Kairotic moment. This refers to a specific event in time or a particular point in time which has great significance for the rest of time. In the history of salvation, the incarnation of Christ would be a kairotic moment. It may be used to refer to a high point in the Christian life, such as coming to faith in Jesus Christ.

Katakein. A Greek word meaning to hold down or suppress. It describes man's suppression of the knowledge of God in

Romans chapter one. Truth is being suppressed in a way that it takes effort to do it.

Kenosis. (emptying oneself) This Greek word is used in Philippians 2:7 stating that Christ "emptied himself." This becomes a heresy when professing Christians claim that Jesus Christ gave up any of His divine attributes. One of the cardinal doctrines of the Christian religion is that God is immutable. God cannot cease to be God. Jesus Christ is God, the second person of the trinity. The correct doctrine is that Christ emptied himself of the manifestations of his glory in his state of humiliation. [See Humiliation of Christ]

Krisis. This is the Greek word for judgment. A judgment requires a decision, therefore to make a judgment is to decide between two concepts, ideas, etc. God's judgment is based on righteousness. The English word crisis comes from the Greek *krisis* indicating the critical nature of judgment. This ultimately refers to the last judgment, the day of the Lord.

Küng, Hans. A Roman Catholic theologian calling for reform in the Church. He is a spokesman for ecumenical unity in the church. He believes there is some truth in all religions.

Kurios/kurion. (Literally means Lord of lords). This New Testament term indicates that Jesus Christ is in a class by himself. He is not merely a king of human lords. "Jesus is *Kurios*" (Lord) was the confession used by the early church in contradistinction to "Caesar is *kurios*" (lord) used by the Romans.

Kuyper, Abraham. (1837-1920) This Dutch theologian, publisher, and politician planted the seeds for a system of apologetics known as presuppositional apologetics. This view of apologetics taken to its logical end teaches that man's total depravity destroyed the ability to reason. [See Presuppositional apologetics]

Law of Choice. (this philosophical concept defined according to Jonathan Edwards' *Freedom of the Will*) The will always chooses according to its strongest inclination at the moment. Human beings choose what they want. Their choices are determined by their desires. [See Will]

Law of God. An expression of God's holiness. God's law reflects his nature and character, especially those attributes of love and justice. The Reformer's categorized God's law as moral, ceremonial, and judicial. God's moral law was summarized by the Lord Jesus Christ in Luke 10:27: "You shall love the LORD your God with all you heart, with all your soul, with all your strength, and with all your mind, and your neighbor as yourself." The Old Testament ceremonial laws expressed in types and figures the future fulfillment of Divine worship in spirit and truth. The Old Testament judicial laws were given to the nation Israel as a formula of justice. The purpose of God's law is threefold. It was given to restrain sin in a sinful world, as a tutor to lead us to Christ, and a rule for Christian life.

Law of non-contradiction. A law of logic that states that contrary properties cannot belong to the same thing, at the same time, and in the same sense. For example God cannot be God and not be God at the same time and in the same relationship. This law is necessary for intelligent human discourse. [See Laws regulating intelligent human discourse]

Law of verification. The verification principle of logical positivism states that no statement or proposition is meaningful unless it can be verified empirically. Ironically, the principle cannot be empirically verified. [See logical positivism; Empiricism]

Laws of immediate inference. Sometimes called the process of immediate inference, it describes the relationship between words like all, each, every, etc. For instance to say that "some" squirrels have tails immediately asserts by inference that it is false to say "no" squirrels have tails.

Laws regulating intelligent human discourse. These non-negotiable principles are necessary for any discussion to make sense. The three absolutes are:

1) The validity of the law of non-contradiction.
2) The validity of the law of causality.
3) The basic reliability of sense perception.

These presuppositions are necessary for science and knowledge. The basis for intelligence is the ability of words to communicate truth. Intelligent discourse depend on these laws. [See Law of non-contradiction; Causality; Sense Perception]

Legal fiction. This is a pejorative term used by the Roman Catholic Church referring to the Reformed view of justification. They say the Reformers claim that Scriptures teach that justification declares someone to be just who is not just. According to Rome the declaration of righteousness is legal and since the person is not actually righteous it is merely a fictious proposition. [See Analytical Justification; Forensic Justification; Justification]

Liberalism.   [See Theological liberalism]

Liberium arbitrium. (free choice) After the Fall man has free will but lacks liberty (*libertas*) which means man is free to choose that which he desires, but lacks the ability to choose righteousness because fallen man only has wicked desires. He is dead in trespasses and sins, which means he cannot incline himself toward the things of God. Fallen man does have rational epistemological abilities. However, his moral decisions are based strictly on self-interest, not obedience based on his love for God.

Limited atonement.   The Calvinistic expression of the particular application of Christ's atonement on behalf of the elect. This expression is applicable only to the saving work of Christ, since all of creation was and will ultimately be affected by the atonement of Christ, either positively or negatively.

Logic.   Although the word logic is not found in Scripture the Greek word *logos* was used in the Greek world to explain mans intellectual relationship to the world. The Bible uses *logos* to explain the ultimate explanation of mans relationship to the world which is found in Jesus Christ. Logic is the way reasonable creatures come to understand who they are in this world. Logic is the way of reason and rational thought. Rational thought is the greatest gift God gave to the human race. Jesus Christ is the greatest gift God gave to those who believe Him for the salvation of their souls. [See *Organon*]

Logical positivism.   Scientific inquiry and logic are the tools of this 20th century school of thought used to develop the verification principle whereby no proposition is meaningful unless it can be verified empirically. [See Law of verification; Empiricism]

Logical priority.   This term is used in connection with the *ordo salutis* (order of salvation).   It describes a necessary condition in the *ordo salutis* (order of salvation). For instance, regeneration must logically come before faith. This stands in distinction to temporal priority. [See Temporal priority; *Ordo salutis*]

Logos. A Greek term indicating discourse or reason. It is used to describe Jesus as the second person of the Trinity as the revealer and revelation of the Father. In Greek thought *logos* is the fundamental concept of all intelligence. [See Logic]

Lord's Supper. Sometimes referred to as communion or the Eucharist, this New Testament sacrament was instituted by the Lord Jesus Christ at the Passover meal the night before His crucifixion. The *Westminster Shorter Catechism* explains that "by giving and receiving bread and wine according to Christ's appointment, his death is showed forth; and the worthy receivers are, not after a corporal and carnal manner, but by faith, made partakers of his body and blood, with all his benefits, to their spiritual nourishment, and growth in grace." The fundamental truth in this sacrament is to remember the Lord Jesus Christ; "Do this in remembrance of Me" (1 Corinthians 11: 24). [See Sacraments]

Love. The Bible uses the word love a variety of different ways, but never gives a clear concrete definition. The Greek words translated love in the New Testament are *phileo* and *agape*. *Phileo* comes from a Greek noun, which is also translated "friend." When Jesus was summoned to come to Bethany to see Lazarus, the sisters of Lazarus said, "he whom you love is sick" (John 11:3). The Greek word in that text is *phileo* that referred to the affection Jesus had for Lazarus. Such is the kind of love that one friend has toward another friend. *Agape* love from the New Testament Greek text tends to reflect the nature of the Christian faith. For instance, Jesus said love your enemies, yet Jesus spoke harshly and unloving toward the Pharisees. When Jesus confronted the young rich ruler he "felt a love" for him, but sent him away without the grace of Christ (Mark 10:21). Agape love expresses God's mercy and compassion whether it means confronting a sinner or comforting a sinner saved by grace. The apostle summarized biblical love in these words: "He who does not love does not know God, for God is love" (1 John 4:8).

Lust.   The typical English usage associates lust with unbridled passions more commonly expressed by inordinate sexual desires. The Greek word translated lust in the New Testament is also used in a good sense, because in Luke 22:15 Jesus said "I have desired to eat this Passover with you before I suffer." The word "desire" is from the same Greek word that is translated lust in the New Testament.   However, most biblical references portray lust as evil. "For all this is in the world the lust of the flesh, the lust of the eyes and the pride of life is not of the Father but is of the world" (1 John 2:16). The common use of the word lust generally expresses the desire to have something that is forbidden by God.

Manifestum.   (clear or conspicuous) This Latin word means plain or obvious.   It is used like the Greek word *phaneros* meaning "revealing" which describes how God has revealed His divine attributes. [See Phaneros]

Marks of the Church.   The development of the 16th century Reformation brought into focus the primary aspect of the church's identity. To distinguish between the true church and the false church, the Reformers believed the church was marked by:

1) The sound preaching of the word of God
2) The proper administration of the sacraments
3) The faithful exercise of church discipline.
These disciplines are for the purpose of reforming the church according to the word of God.   They are not intended to tyrannize God's people. [See Reformation]

Marx, Karl.   A 19th century philosopher who opposed Hegelian philosophy. He believed Hegel missed the root cause of all tension and struggle. According to Marx, philosophy was not a conflict over ideas, but over material goods. [See Dialectical Materialism]

Mass. A Roman Catholic sacrament that claims to offer a fresh sacrifice of Christ each time it is administered. [See Lord's Supper; Sacraments]

Mechanical dictation. This is a false view of the inspiration of Scripture. According to this view the Bible writers were like the keys of a typewriter, simply following the command of the one pressing the keys. This view looses the personality of the writer. [See Inspiration]

Mediate general revelation. The revelation of God which comes through some medium, such as the created order. [See General revelation; Immediate general revelation]

Mediator. One who attempts to reconcile two parties in conflict. In the Old Testament the priest was the mediator between God and man prefiguring the true Mediator, the Lord Jesus Christ. As the God-man Jesus Christ represents both sides God and man.

Melchizedek. [See Priesthood of Melchizedek]

Metaphysics. That which is beyond the scope of this physical world. Christians use this term to describe the ultimate reality of being beyond this world. This word often avoided by Christian leaders (preachers, teachers, counselors, etc.) is necessary to make the distinction between the sacred and the secular.

Meritum de congruo. (*congruos* merit, half merit) The

view that God rewards good deeds not because justice requires it, but because it is fitting. This is an act of divine grace, even though God was not required to reward it. Man cannot do anything to deserve God's grace.

Meritum de condigno. (*condign* merit, full merit) This merit necessarily imposes a reward from a just judge.

Mind. In Christian theology, this is the metaphysical aspect of the soul that is the center of reason, intelligence, and understanding. The mind of God is perfect unlike the mind of sinful man. The Bible uses the Greek word *nous* to describe the condition of humanity without God (Romans 1:28). The Bible also uses a word connected with *nous* to describe the human ability to understand God by the power of the mind (Romans 1:20). The physical brain will cease to exist, but the mind will remain forever. [See Soul; Noetic effect of sin]

Miracle. An effect that is derived from a supernatural cause. The word miracle found in the Bible may be traced to the Greek words *semeion* and *dunamis*. *Semeion* is normally translated "sign" and *dunamis* is normally translated "power." A biblical miracle is a sign of God's power which proves God's authority and validates the entire corpus of Scripture.

Modalism. A heretical doctrine of the Trinity. The three parts of the trinity (Father, Son, Holy Spirit) are modes of God's activity rather than three distinct persons.

Modalistic Monarchianism. A heresy which stresses the unity of God. This teaches that Christ was the manifestation of God in the Old Testament and the Holy Spirit after Pentecost.

Modern mysticism. This concept is often employed to

describe faith as a blind faith instead of having faith in some objective reality. Biblical faith insists that something must be "known" if something is to be "believed." [See Faith]

Modernity. A cultural concept that links the character and system of the world to the forces of modernization and technology that produce it. This concept encompasses many world and life views and is not necessarily limited to a specific period in history although many believe that the greatest impact began with the storming of the Bastille in the 18th century and lasted until the emergence of postmodernity in the middle of the 20th century. However, its presence will remain until some unknown time in the future.

Monergism. This term consists of two Greek words *mono* which means alone or only and *ergo* which means to work. It describes the Augustinian view that regeneration is the work of God only or the alone work of God. The Jonathan Edwards scholar Perry Miller, is believed to have coined the phrase, "the holy rape of the soul" to describe the alleged view of the Puritans. The unregenerate sinner is morally unable to believe and trust Christ alone for eternal salvation except by a monergistic intrusion of the Holy Spirit. [See Regeneration]

Monogenes. (only begotten) A Greek word used in John 1:14 et al. to describe the uniqueness of Jesus Christ as begotten, not made. This describes the relationship between God the Father and God the Son.

Monophysite heresy. A Christological heresy that followed the Council of Chalcedon (451). This teaching, primarily in the Eastern Church, was that Jesus Christ had only one nature in which the human became divine in a single theanthropic nature. [See Chalcedonian formulation; Theantrophic nature]

Monotheism. (One God) This term is used to describe a personal transcendent God who is the God over all. Judiasm and Christianity embrace this doctrine and reject polytheism (More than one God). The historical critical belief is that everything moves from the simple to the complex so that monotheism finally triumphs over polytheism. [See Henotheism; Polytheism]

Moral ability. According to Jonathan Edwards, moral ability refers to the power to perform either good or evil. [See moral inability; Natural ability]

Moralism. This worldview adopted by many evangelicals tends to make moral perfection the Christian standard for salvation. Moralism belongs to the doctrine of sanctification. The biblical doctrine of sanctification teaches the justification by faith alone breaks the dominion of sin, but sin is not eradicated. Self-righteousness is the platform for moralism. It is the modern concept for perfectionism. The Christian worldview is moral, but not perfect.

Moral inability. According to Jonathan Edwards, fallen man is born into sin and does not have the power to choose righteousness unless regenerated By Christ. [See Moral ability; Natural ability]

Mortal sin. The Roman Catholic Church teaches that this sin kills justifying grace in the soul. This sin results from disobedience to the Ten Commandments with a knowledgeable perversion and deliberate intention to destroy the love of God poured into the heart.

Moses redivinus. (*Redivinus* means come back to life) In Deuteronomy. 18:15, this refers to Christ as a prophet like Moses, the second lawgiver.

Munus triplex. (threefold office) A Christological term referring to the threefold work of Christ as prophet, priest, and king. All three of these Old Testament offices were fulfilled by Christ. This concept was most clearly defined by John Calvin.

Muratorian Council. A church council in 398 A.D. that determined what books would be received into the canon of Holy Scripture. [See Canon]

Mystery. The Greek word in the New Testament, *musterion*, translated mystery does not refer to something unknowable, but it is that which God has chosen not to reveal at any particular time to any particular people. Luther said it was God's inscrutable or unsearchable will.

Mysterium tremendum. (overwhelming mystery) A term used by Rudolph Otto in "Idea of the Holy". When people approach that which is holy the natural response is fear and trembling. [See Idea of the Holy; Otto, Rudolph]

Natural ability. Jonathan Edwards believed that man has the ability to think, to move, and communicate, and to choose, though limited by his own nature which after the fall is a sinful nature. [See Moral ability; Moral inability]

Natural Law. This term derived from the Bible states that unbelievers "who do not have the law, by nature do the things in the law" (Romans 2:14). In philosophy it is also referred to as a "higher law." In theology, the law of God, summarized in the Ten Commandments, is the basis for natural law. It establishes the standard of ethics in reality. The law of God is part of the rational creature. Natural man is in a state of moral dependency, thus natural law saves natural man from self-destruction.

Natural theology.   The proposition that some knowledge of God can be derived from the natural world. Natural theology is insufficient for salvation. The knowledge of God and His divine attributes can be known from creation (Romans 1:20 and Romans 2:14-15).

Nestorianism. This heresy taught by Nestorius separated the divine and human natures so that two persons existed in a dual personality. It was condemned in Ephesus in 431 A. D. [See Chalcedonian formulation]

Neo-orthodoxy.   A reaction against liberal Protestantism. Karl Barth was a major proponent who allegedly rescued the Bible from the higher critics and re-established it as important for faith once again. This view says the Bible is a human witness of a revelational experience.   This quickly degenerated into liberalism. [See Barth, Karl]

New Birth.   [See Regeneration]

Nicea.   A church council in 325 A.D. which condemned Arianism and formulated the orthodox doctrine of the Trinity. [See Arianism; Trinity]

Noetic effect of sin.   The Greek word *nous* essentially refers to the mind, reason, or understanding. The word *noetic* comes from the Greek word *nous*. The *noetic* effect of sin refers to the mind, so the question must be asked: to what extent did the fall of man affect the mind?   The *noetic* structure (the function of the mind) refers to the sum total of everything a person knows and consequently believes. For instance, Adam's ability to reason before the Fall was like the rest of creation; it was perfect. The *noetic* effect of sin did not destroy reason, but rather defaced it. [See Mind]

Nominalism. (From the Latin word *nominalis*, meaning "pertaining to names") This is a term used in the study of epistemology (theory of knowledge). Its origin from early Greek philosophy was that universal concepts were merely names and therefore were not metaphysical realities. As with all concepts of philosophy, there will be theological implications. The implications of this theory of knowledge to the western world have serious consequences for Christian theology. If there are no metaphysical realities, then faith becomes the only meaningful explanation for reality. Therefore, the God-given rational mind serves no purpose. The next step is to dismiss the meaning of words and adopt the postmodern hermeneutic. [See Hermeneutics]

Non posse non peccare. (not able to not sin) Augustine used this term to describe the condition of man after the Fall, but does not apply to Jesus Christ. [See Augustinianism]

Non posse peccare. (not able to sin) Augustine used this term to describe the condition of the elect in the final state of glory. There the elect will not be able to sin. [See Augustinianism]

Nose of wax. Martin Luther used this term to describe the improper use of hermeneutics; treating scripture as something which can be shaped to say what we wish it to say. [See Hermeneutics]

Notitia. (knowledge) The 16th century Reformers used this word to explain *sola fide* (faith alone). Faith must have content, therefore the mind must be involved. This is the first of the three elements necessary for faith which denote the content, or object of faith. [See Faith; Assensus; Fiducia]

Noumenal world.   This term coined by Immanuel Kant describes that which cannot be apprehended through the senses. Kant puts God, self, and essences in the *noumenal* world. [See Kant, Immanuel; Phenomenal world]

Omnipotent.   This theological term comes from two Latin words *omni potens* meaning all and powerful.   This term describes that attribute of God who has sovereign power and authority over all creation. It is one of the principal doctrines of the Christian religion.

Omnipresence.   This term comes from two Latin words *omni praesent* meaning everywhere present.   God is a Spirit and is not limited by physics.   [See Immensity of God; Ubiquity]

Omniscience.   This term comes from two Latin words *omni scientia* meaning all knowledge.   It refers to God's ability to know everything, past, present, and future.   Theologians are particularly divided over this doctrine, because it is said to deprive man of his free will.

Ontology.   That part of philosophy that deals with the nature of being as being.   It is a rational analysis of the necessary and universal aspects of being. The doctrine of being stands in contrast to the doctrine of becoming (signifying some change) and the doctrine of nothing.   Standing at the head of all being is God Himself, the model of all perfection and goodness.   [See Parmenides]

Opiate of the masses.   (opiate refers to the drug opium) This is how Karl Marx explained religion.   He believed that capitalists invented the idea of God to keep the poor in their place and used religion to promote their agenda.   Free market theists, figuratively speaking, sedated the people with propaganda. [See Marx, Karl]

Ordo salutis. (order of salvation) It refers to the logical order of the causes and effects which produce salvation. The different aspects of the *ordo salutis* are election, calling, regeneration, conversion (including repentance and faith), justification, adoption, sanctification, and glorification. [See Salvation]

Organon. This Greek word refers to a tool or an instrument. A term used by students of Aristotle to describe logic, which is the *organon* (instrument) of all sciences. Subsequent philosophers and theologians believe it is necessary for all meaningful and intelligible discourse. It contains no content, but is the principle by which all content is ordered. [Logic]

Orge. (wrath) A Greek word found in Romans 1:18 usually translated "wrath" but has the sense of unbridled raging wrath. This Greek word seems to summarize Romans chapter one that teaches that man "exchanged the truth of God for the lie" and that the "wrath (*orge*) of God is revealed."

Original righteousness. This refers to the righteousness of Adam and Eve before the Fall. This was not a condition of neutrality, because they were created good, but not consummately good.

Original sin. The result or effect of the sin of Adam. The *Westminster Shorter Catechism* describes it as "the want of original righteousness, and the corruption of his whole nature." This is God's actual judgment on the human race.

Orthodoxy. (from the Greek word *orthos* meaning right and *doxa* meaning opinion, thus having the right opinion) This generally refers to the fundamental tenets of the Christian religion. For instance an orthodox view of Christ is that He was very God and very man in two distinct natures, but one person. The orthodox Christian religion begins with a belief in the triune nature of God, the authority of Scripture, the person and work of Jesus Christ, and the bodily return of Jesus Christ to judge the world. There are degrees of orthodoxy within the Christian religion. The Apostles' Creed establishes an orthodox doctrine for a much larger segment of the body of Christ than a more specific creed such as the *Westminster Confession of Faith*. This word stands in contrast to heterodoxy which means "other opinion." [See Heresy]

Otto, Rudolph. (1869-1937) This German scholar best defined the cultural sense of the holy. He was not interested in studying God, but studied how cultures respond to that which they consider to be sacred. [See Idea of the Holy; Mysterium tremendum]

Paedocommunion. A term that defines the practice of permitting young children to come to the Lord's Supper who are too young to discern the Lord's body.

Panentheism. Process theologians teach that God is part of all creation, but God transcends creation as He changes and develops. [See Process theology]

Pantheism. This comes from a Greek word, which means everything is God. It is world and life view used by some world religions to teach that all nature is divine.

Para-church movement. This refers to a mixture of organizations and agencies that claim some relationship to some aspect of the work of the church. There are more than 10,000 such organizations and agencies in the United States. The Dictionary of Christianity in America defines a parachurch organization as a "voluntary, not-for-profit association of Christians working outside denominational control to achieve some specific ministry or social service." The Bible has no allowance for such an organization.

Paradox. (appears to be something else) This refers to something that seems to be contradictory, but under close scrutiny is not contradictory.

Parmenides. A Greek philosopher who believed in pure being. He thought a philosopher should not talk nonsense. He became famous for the saying: "What is, is." The philosophical concept has theological implications, especially relative to essence and existence. [See Essence; Existence; Existere; Ontology]

Partial inerrancy. Some neo-orthodox theologians believe that the Bible contains, in specified places, revelation from God. [See Neo-orthodoxy]

Passive obedience. The term passive is not a reference to Christ being inactive in His obedience, but rather it refers to His obedience in suffering the Father's wrath on behalf of the elect.

Patripassianism. (the passions or suffering of the Father) This was the name given to the Modalistic Monarchians (Christ was a temporary form of the one God) by Cyprian. This view teaches that the Father came in the person of Christ, therefore the Father suffered and died. [See Modalistic monarchianism]

Peace. This biblical concept describes the state of the soul in relation to God. The relationship of man to God after the fall, but before regeneration is war. The Bible describes this war as the "wrath of God" (Romans 1:18). The justifying work of Christ applied to the soul of man is that condition that brings peace. The end of war is peace accompanied by freedom from strife, disputes and dissensions.

Pelagianism. Pelagius (383-410) argued that the fall of the human race was nothing more than a historical event that affected Adam alone. Moral ability was not affected by the Fall. Therefore, humans are born free of sin and they are able to sin or not to sin. They are able to obey the Law without grace and to resist heaven. This view denies the doctrine of original sin. [See Moral ability; Moral inability; Natural ability; Original sin]

Penance. This is a sacrament of the Roman Catholic Church given to those who have committed mortal sin. It involves:

1) confession,
2) contrition,
3) priestly absolution
4) works of satisfaction.

It is referred to as the second plank of justification for those who have made shipwreck of their souls.

Personification. This is a literary device where personal characteristics are assigned to non-human objects. For instance the Bible says, "Let the rivers clap their hands" (Psalm 98:8). Rivers do not have hands, but the representation is found in the context of God's salvation bringing joy to all creation.

Perspicuity of the Scriptures. (perspicuity is the ability to see through or be transparent) This refers to the clarity of

Scripture. Does not mean that each part of Scripture is equally clear, but the meaning is discernible.

Persuasion. An experience that is distinct from proof. Persuasion is not proof. Persuasion is the result of sound evidence. For instance, the *Westminster Confession of Faith* says, "the word of God does abundantly evidence itself to be the word of God." However, our full persuasion "is from the inward work of the Holy Spirit."

Phaneros. (visible or manifest) A Greek word used in Romans 1:19 which means manifest or evident. In that text it is used in connection with the wrath of God manifested or clearly seen in General Revelation. [See Manifestum]

Phenomenal world. (appears to our sensation) Immanuel Kant claims that we are not able to move from the visible to the invisible. This is the world we live in and understand from our senses. The other world, the *noumenal* world includes God, self, and essences. [See Noumenal world; Kant]

Philosophy. (derived from two Greek words, *philos*, meaning friend and *sophos*, meaning wise) This term literally refers to a "friend of wisdom." The acquisition of knowledge combined with experience is a condition for wisdom. God gives all His children wisdom through mediate sources, but may grant wisdom immediately in extraordinary ways. Every Christian is a philosopher (a friend of wisdom) in the right sense. "Wisdom is the principle thing; Therefore get wisdom. And in all your getting, get understanding" (Proverbs 4:7). Philosophy is true or false. God expects His children to acquire true philosophy, and dismiss false philosophy.

Plenary verbal inspiration. This view of the inspiration of Scripture teaches that God inerrantly and infallibly superintended the men who wrote the words of Holy Scripture so that the original manuscripts were without any error. [See Inerrant; Infallibility]

Plural of majesty.   (Referring to the Hebrew word *Elohim*) The plural form of the Hebrew word *Elohim* translated into English as God is used to express the intensity of God's majesty. It indicates the fullness of God's majesty. It is a reference to royalty and the ultimate authority of God. Some theologians believe the reference to "Us" in Genesis 1:26 is a plural of majesty, while others believe it refers to the Trinity.

Pluralism.   The philosophical meaning is the belief that the world was made out of different elements. The concept of multiple elements in one world has led many to embrace a diversity of world religions, all of which lead to the truth of God.

Polytheism.   Taken from the Greek word *polus* meaning "many" and *theos* meaning "god." The concept of multiple gods developed as a religious concept. The historical critical school believed everything moved from the simple to the complex. This is the second stage where god has his or her own role or particular function. [See Henotheism]

Posse non peccare.   (able to not sin) Augustine used this term to describe Adam before the Fall and regenerated man. The regenerated man is able to sin, but also able not to sin. [See Augustinianism]

Posse peccare.   (able to sin) Augustine used this term to describe Adam before the Fall. This also describes regenerated man since he is able to sin, but it also describes regenerate man who is also able not to sin. [See Augustinianism]

Postmillennialism.   The belief that Jesus will come again after a golden age of 1,000 years on earth. It holds that Christ will, through the work of His church, exercise dominion over all the earth during the millennium. The millennium is not perfect but a time when the Christian faith prevails in the culture and dominates the thinking of the world. There are at least two very distinct subdivisions of those who claim this term. The broadest historical group are simply those who believe that the world is going to get better and better, culminating in the millennium, and then the return of Christ. The second group began with the rise of theological liberalism. This variety essentially denied the work of the Spirit bringing the millennium and saw it as a result of the application of education, the rise of modernity and assorted programs of social change.   [Amillennialism; Eschatology; Premillennialism]

Postmodernity.   The term itself implies that the concept inferred is beyond the modern. It is more of a conceptual idea than a period of time. The postmodern concept seems to have emerged around the middle of the twentieth century by rejecting the traditional establishment and subjectively interpreting reality. The postmodern has challenged modern architecture, theories in law, education, and science as well as establishing a new method of interpreting literature called deconstructionism. [See Deconstructionism]

Postestas absolutas.   (absolute power) This Latin phrase refers to God's absolute power and sovereignty. Since it means absolute power and because God is absolute power, He is the law. When used in conjunction with *ex lex* it means God is all powerful and outside the law. Some theologians try to make a distinction between the absolute and ordained power of God to resolve any contingencies or conflict with the will. [See Ex lex controversy]

Power of the keys.   The Roman Catholic doctrine that the Pope is the vicar of Christ on earth, therefore he has the power of remission of temporal guilt and the power to punish evildoers.

Pragmatism.   This is the practical worldview. If the theory produces results, then it must be true. If it works it must be right. It dismisses all metaphysical and rational concepts, if they do not appear to be productive in the eyes of the observer.

Preceptive will of God.   This refers to what God wills that Christians should do.   According to Francis Turretin the decretive will of God is distinct from the perceptive will. His decretive will is what God ordains by decree. His precepts are found in His law and may be clearly understood, but His decretive will is a mystery to mankind. [See Decretive will of God]

Predestination.   The biblical doctrine that teaches the ultimate destiny of all created things was fixed by God before the creation of the world. This doctrine shows the absolute authority of God over all of creation. The fall of man destined all of humanity to everlasting punishment, but it is the loving sovereign plan of God to save all those who turn to Him in faith and repentance.

Premillennialism.   The view that Jesus Christ will return to earth and establish an earthly kingdom and reign for one thousand years. The role of the anti-christ and the period of tribulation varies among the premillennialists. This particular view takes a literal approach to the interpretation of the book of Revelation, especially chapter twenty, which is the only clear and explicit teaching of the millennium in Scripture. [See Amillennialism; Chiliasm; Eschatology; Postmillennialism]

Presuppositional apologetics. The basic idea is that biblical revelation is the presupposition upon which any coherent system of truth must be built. However, there are three varieties of presuppositionalism.

1) <u>Gordon Clarke's presuppositionalism.</u>

He believes that Scripture is the source of all truth. Since God has revealed Himself in Scripture, these axioms are the starting point for inquiry into truth.

2) <u>Cornelius Van Til's presuppositionalism.</u>

It may be argued that his starting point was God as He is found in Scripture. According to presuppositionalism there is no epistimological common ground for the believer and unbeliever.

3) <u>Ronald Nash's presuppositionalism.</u>

Nash claims in his book *Faith and Reason* that his method only provides probability and in his own words "To demand logical certainty in the matters under consideration in this book [apologetics is under consideration] is bizarre. My admission that we must deal in terms of probabilities (in the logical sense) is not a defect..." (Faith and Reason, pages 65-66) [See Apologetics; Kuyper, Abraham]

Prescient view of election. (to know before) This is the Arminian response to the doctrine of election and predestination. This view teaches that God knows from all eternity who will believe on Jesus Christ and who will reject Christ. The doctrine of election from this perspective is based on God's foreknowledge of human choices. This is not consistent with the doctrine of predestination as it is taught in Scripture because the ultimate sovereign in salvation according to this teaching is man, not God. [See Predestination]

Preterist. This is the interpretative theory used by those who believe that the events described in the book of Revelation have already occurred. This view makes the book very important for those who originally received the letter, but less meaningful to later generations except for the facts of those days in the early church. [See Eschatology; Futurist; Historicist]

Prevenient grace. (prevenient means "to come before") Roman Catholics and Protestant Arminians join hands affirming that God gives all men a grace that comes before regeneration, so that man is enabled to cooperate with God in the work of regeneration. Obviously, prevenient grace is also associated with the concept of a universal atonement.

Pride. The Bible speaks of pride often as a condition of the heart, but does not actually give a specific definition. The word is often used in conjunction with synonyms like contempt, arrogance, and boasting. Pride appears to be a root sin and therefore the mother of many other sins. Pride is the opposite of humility, contentment, and modesty. Judgment is often the companion of pride. "Pride goes before destruction, and a haughty spirit before a fall" (Proverbs 16:18).

Priesthood of Melchizedek. Melchizedek was a priest/king of Salem. Abraham (the subordinate) paid tithes to Melchizedek and he blessed Abraham. Abraham is greater than Levi and Melchizedek is greater than Abraham, therefore Melchizedek is greater than Levi. Many theologians regard him as a type of Christ.

Primary cause. God is the ultimate cause of everything that occurs. God ordained everything that comes to pass, including the means which are secondary causes. This important doctrine is a source of great controversy because the unbelievers claim God ordained sin and therefore God is the cause of sin. Therefore man is not responsible for his or her sin. The Bible says, "God cannot be tempted by evil, nor does He Himself tempt anyone" (James 1:13). The author of this article responds: no one to my satisfaction has resolved this issue but it remains a mystery which does not violate the law of non-contradiction. [See Mystery; Theodicy]

Principle of private interpretation. Every Christian has the right to interpret the Bible without being bound to the interpretation of the church. [See Hermeneutics; Analogy of faith]

Process theology. A heresy which affirms that God is in the process of change. The central idea is that reality is a process of becoming. This heresy was popularized under the language of God's "openness" by Clark Pinnock. [See Panentheism]

Procrustean Bed. Allusion to a character in Greek mythology where Procrustes was put in a bed that was too short for him. To solve the problem, Procrustes' feet were cut off. The concept is to force something to fit specific criteria when it really doesn't. This concept is often used in interpreting Scripture.

Progressive revelation. Classical orthodox view of revelation which demonstrates the progress of redemption. The concept of soteriology (doctrine of salvation) is progressively expanding throughout God's covenant.

Promise keepers. A parachurch movement which defines its mission as that "to unite men who are separated by race, geography, culture, denomination, and economics." It has assumed to itself the responsibility given specifically to the church. [See Parachurch movement]

Proof.　In theology and philosophy proof is the substance necessary to demonstrate fully and compellingly the truth of a proposition.

Propitiation.　This is a satisfaction of divine justice. Jesus Christ satisfied God's divine wrath against His elect. [See Expiation]

Protagoras.　The Greek philosopher credited as founding father of humanism. He coined the Greek term *homo mensura* which means "man is the measure of all things." [See Homo mensura]

Providence.　(From the Latin word *providere* meaning to see in advance, therefore preparing in advance) God has ordained events so that good will be the final result. There are four dimensions to the providence of God.

1. Sustenance - God sustains what He creates. Everything in the universe is dependent on the being and power of God.

2. Provision - God not only creates, but he provides for all things based on his foreordination of all things. His ultimate provision is His Son, Jesus Christ, the only Redeemer of the elect.

3. Government - God governs the world by his absolute authority and power. He has the right and ability to govern all things that come to pass.

4. Concurrence - It literally means to run together with. Used in connection with the doctrine of God's providence, it is used when describing the primary and secondary causes and that they

operate concurrently. God's purpose is brought to pass by his sovereignty even though he uses human means. An example of the doctrine of concurrence is found in Genesis where the brothers of Joseph (Gen. 37-50) did evil, but God meant it for good.

Provision. God not only creates, but he provides for all things based on his foreordination of all things. His ultimate provision is His Son, Jesus Christ, the only Redeemer of the elect. [See Providence]

Pseudepigrapha. (false writings) This refers to the books rejected by the church as inspired books of the New Testament. The book of Enoch and the gospel of Barnabas are a couple of examples. [See Canon]

Pure actuality. Refers to the inherent powers a thing possessed by virtue of its being the kind of things it is. In theology God is pure actuality and has no potentiality.

Purgatory. The Roman Catholic Church believes this is the place of the purging of sins for those who died in a state of grace. People pay for venial sins in purgatory. When they are paid in full, they go to heaven. [See Venial sin]

Queen of the Sciences. This was a reference to theology during the medieval period in church history because it was that which unified all the diversity of reality. There was a time when many universities had schools of theology, but now they are called schools of religion, thus abandoning the centrality of God in education. [See University]

Rationalism. A theory of philosophy in which the criterion of truth is not sensory but intellectual and deductive. Rationalism is a worldview that worships reason as its god. However, rational describes the quality necessary for intelligent communication. A rational creature is a reasonable creature. Although sin distorted the rational abilities of the human race, it did not destroy rationality. Rationalism is the opposite of empiricism. [See Empiricism; Reason]

Reason. God's gift to the human race that gives humans the ability to think rationally, and therefore intelligently. Reason is the ground of intellectual ability and the seat of all knowledge. [See Logic]

Recipemus. (we receive) This was a key word used at the Muratorian council to explain that the church received the books of Scripture. The church acknowledges its subordination to the Bible and the Bible's authority. [Muratorian Council]

Reconciliation. Man was created in the image of God, but man's sin disenfranchised him from a favorable relation with God. We are reconciled with God through the death of Jesus Christ and His atoning sacrifice. Reconciliation will be the result of forgiveness. If one Christian forgives another Christian, they must be reconciled. [See Forgiveness]

Reconstructionism. When applied to Christianity this term generally refers to theonomy and to some aspect of postmillennialism eschatology. [See Postmillennialism; Eschatology; Theonomy]

Reductionism. A term used when one aspect of something is considered and all the other aspects are ignored. A frequent mistake in biblical interpretation. [See Hermeneutics; Nose of wax]

Reformation. Relative to the 16th century Reformation it began as a protest initially of a few theologians and eventually of a large number of Christians who wanted to see the Roman Catholic Church reform doctrine to be more consistent with Scripture. Two chief causes of the Reformation:

1) Formal cause - *Sola Scriptura* (Scripture alone) Luther asked by what other authority he would debate the issue of justification by faith alone. Scripture alone is infallible and no authority can bind the conscience.

2) Material cause - *Sola Fide* (Faith alone) The argument of justification by faith alone done with no mixture of human effort to accomplish justification.

Regeneration. The sovereign efficacious act of the Holy Spirit so that the elect are given new life in Jesus Christ and enabled to understand and embrace the law and the gospel for the saving of their soul. The Holy Spirit operates by divine initiative to give those who are dead in sin new life in Christ. Regeneration is necessary before faith. [See Efficacy]

Reification of doctrine. The term means "to make impersonal" when it is used in connection with Neo-orthodoxy. They would say the Bible does not have any concrete meaning without a personal encounter by revelation from Jesus Christ or through the Scriptures as they become the word of God. [See Neo-orthodoxy]

Repentance. The common use of this word in the New Testament refers to the change of one's mind. The change of mind calls the sinner to believe God and to turn from his sin to God with the purpose of obeying God's commandments because of his love for God.

Revelation. Refers to the disclosure or unveiling of something. There are two ways God reveals Himself to His rational creatures: General and Special Revelation.

General revelation. Refers to the scope (audience, whole world) and content of God making himself known. Furthermore, it is less specific and not salvific (being an instrument of salvation).

Special revelation. God reveals himself as defined in the Bible and demonstrated through the person of Christ.

Immediate general revelation. Certain knowledge of God which man can know by innate knowledge which God puts in man. God's self disclosure without any medium. The following are helpful distinctives.

Mediate general revelation - Revelation that is given to us through some medium. Specifically God's self-disclosure through creation.

Progressive revelation - The classical orthodox view of the progress of redemption. The concept of soteriology is progressively expanding through God's covenant.

Sufficiency of general revelation - God's revelation of Himself in creation is sufficient for the human race to see their sinfulness in comparison to God's holiness (See Romans 1:18-20), but not sufficient for redemption.

Sabellianism. This heresy taught by Sabellius (3rd century) affirmed a modal Trinity where God is one being or person, but He takes the form of three different modes. This false teaching has visited the church throughout the history of the church such as some modern Pentecostal groups. [See Patripassianism; Modalism]

Sacerdotalism. The doctrine that says the real instrument of salvation is the church. The power is vested to the church by Christ and the church gives authority to the priests who administer the sacraments as a means of salvation. [See Sacraments]

Sacraments. The Latin word *sacramentum* and the Greek word *musterion* reminds Christians of the mystery associated with this sacred duty and means of God's grace. The two sacraments given to the New Testament church are baptism and the Lord's Supper according to Reformed theology. Some denominations such as Southern Baptist do not believe or practice the sacraments. The sacraments are visible signs, seals, and pledges that refers to the mysterious invisible work of God's grace in the life of the believer. The Shorter Catechism defines a sacrament as "a holy ordinance instituted by Christ; wherein, by sensible signs Christ and the benefits of the New Covenant are represented, sealed, and applied to believers." [See Baptism; Lord's Supper; Sacramentum]

Sacramentum. (sacraments) The sacraments are a means of grace the Lord gives through signs and seals for the covenant community. The impact of the sacraments affect how Christians relate to God and to each other.

Salvation. The inspired apostle Paul spoke of salvation in terms of the saving power of Jesus Christ. "For God has not destined us for wrath, but for obtaining salvation through our Lord Jesus Christ..." (1 Thessalonians 5:9). Salvation is not something that belongs to human beings because the Bible says "Salvation belongs to the Lord; Thy blessing be upon Thy people!" (Psalm 3:8). Properly stated salvation is God's gracious hand saving His people for His glory. [See Soteriology]

Sanctification. The saved sinner is in the process of being made righteous. Christianity holds that while we are judged righteous by God the moment we trust in the atoning work of Christ, and that atoning work of Christ is the basis of that judgment, nevertheless believers all grow in grace. They become progressively more like what God judges them to be. We become, in ourselves (though not by ourselves) less sinful, more righteous. This work in man is synergistic, a cooperative work between the individual and the Holy Spirit, who works in us both to will and to do His good pleasure. The process proceeds at different rates with different believers, but with all Christians it does indeed proceed. The process is complete when the believer leaves this life. This doctrine does not teach that the Christian must be pure sometime before death, but that at the death of the Christian the process is brought to its end and the Christian is glorified. [See Simul justis et peccator]

Sartre, Jean Paul. (1905-1980) A French philosopher and leader in existential philosophy. His view of human freedom states that if man does not have total freedom then man does not have any freedom. Any constraints and man is not free. He believed that human autonomy is incompatible with God's sovereignty, which led him to theological despair and philosophical existentialism. [See Existentialism]

Secondary causes. God ordains (as the First Cause) and His will is brought to pass through the actions of secondary causes which have real causal power. For instance, God ordains (First Cause) the pecan to fall from the tree, but it is second causes like rain, wind, and gravity the brings the pecan to the ground as God ordained it. [See Causality]

Secularism. The word secular is a good and useful word which refers to "the present time" or "the here and now." Humanism is the belief that the measure of all things is the human being which is merely a secular being. Therefore humanism measures all things according to the secular. Hence, secular humanism is nothing more that atheism. The negative aspects of these terms must not abscond the proper role of the human created in the image of God and the present time, which God gave for the manifestation of His glory. [See Homo mensura; Protagoras]

Seeking. An aspect of evangelism according to Jonathan Edwards, wherein the lost seek to avail themselves of the means of grace, specifically, the preaching of the word. "The proper method of seeking involves man's doing all this is within his natural power" (Rational Biblical Theology of Jonathan Edwards, vol. 3, p. 50).

Self Authenticating Scripture. Calvin says the Bible has within itself overwhelming evidence of its nature, antiquity, and prophecy. The Word of God would not make a false statement about itself. [See Revelation]

Self determination. All choices are determined by the individual and therefore have a moral dimension. There is a determinate factor which is within all people. [See Will]

Self evident truth. This refers to a proposition that requires no further evidence to verify its truth. Consciousness accompanied by reason will bring about intelligent discourse, which demonstrates truth without the need of arguments.

Semi-Pelagianism. This theological concept is associated with Arminianism. According to the semi-Pelagian Adam's sin had a serious consequence on all his descendants and their wills are significantly weakened, but not rendered incapable of doing good and therefore the morally sick person may respond positively to God's command to repent and believe. [See Will]

Sense perception.   This is used relative to empirical data. The awareness of the external experiences in this world based on the information received from the senses. [See Empiricism]

Sensus divinatatus.   (sense of the divine) A term used by Calvin to explain that man, having innate, immediate revelation of God, is capable only of leaving himself without excuse in his rejection of God's truth. Calvin said, "There is within the human mind, and indeed by natural instinct, an awareness of divinity" (*Institutes of the Christian Religion*, 1.3.1).   [See Natural Theology]

Sensus literalis.   (Literal sense) This term was used by the Reformers to describe "the literal sense of Scripture." The Bible is to be interpreted according to the sense in which it was written.

Sessio.   (from the Latin word *sedo* meaning to sit) The first and most important aspect of this word is the sitting of Christ at the right hand of the Father. It is the position by which He is seated at the seat of judgment. It is used in the Latin text of the Apostles Creed in reference to Jesus sitting on the right hand of God the Father.

Simul justus et peccator.   (at once righteous and a sinner) This Reformation concept explains the relationship between regeneration, justification, and sanctification and the human sinful condition. Martin Luther used this expression to indicate that the justified sinner is just synthetically because Christ's righteousness has been added to the sinner, but at the same time the sinner is a sinner analytically.   Careful study of this theological concept is necessary to understand the paradox. Professor John Murray explained this to mean that "sin remains, but sin does not reign."   [See Justification; Sanctification; Paradox]

Simple being.   This means God is not a compound being or made up of distinct parts. This refers to God's being (essence), not His personhood. [See Compound being; Trinity]

Sin.   The origin of sin can be traced to Adam's disobedience in the Garden of Eden. Adam's sin was unbelief and rebellion accompanied by pride, lust, and covetousness. Since Adam acted as the federal head or the legal representative for the entire human race his sin infected the entire human race. The concept of federal theology is profoundly biblical as the inspired apostle Paul makes it very clear that "through one man's offense [Adam's sin] judgment came to all men, resulting in condemnation . . ." (Romans 5:18). Adam's sin was sufficient to require the condemnation of the entire human race. The corruption conveyed to the human race refers to the moral pollution, which remains throughout this life. The grace of justification removes the guilt and the work of sanctification washes away the moral pollution by the most powerful work of the Holy Spirit. [See Federal theology]

Sola fide.   (by faith alone) The article of the Reformation by which the gospel stands or falls. *Sola fide* is the doctrine that justifies the Christian by trusting in the atoning work of Christ alone. The Reformers taught that faith is the alone instrument of justification. This along with *sola scriptura* was one of the primary causes of the 16th century Reformation. [See Reformation]

Sola scriptura.   (by Scripture alone) The Reformation cry that Scripture alone is the authoritative Word of God. This along with *sola fide* was one of the primary causes of the 16th century Reformation. [See Reformation]

Son of Man.   A title of Christ which emphasizes His deity.

Christ refers to this title in reference to Himself more than any of His other titles.

Sophism. In early Greek philosophy, sophism was a specious argument used to deceive someone. Sophistry is a subtle false argument. To sophisticate means to mislead by deception and false arguments. To be sophisticated is actually bad, although a revised contemporary meaning is that a sophisticated person is worldly wise, mature, classy, in the know, and on top of all situations. If the root word "Sophism" is an enemy to truth, how can its derivative word "sophisticated" be good for truth?   For instance, worldly wise does not necessarily express truth.

Soteriology.   (doctrine of salvation) A discipline within the study of theology that is especially concerned with God's plan for the salvation of the elect. [See Salvation; Ordo salutis]

Soul.   This word found often in the Old and Testaments describes the entity that essentially belongs to human beings forever. Historically western philosophy has treated the soul as a spiritual dimension of humanity.   It appears that modern psychology locates the soul in some physical substance, since they often prescribe drugs that alter the brain function. Although theologians have serious disagreements on the meaning of the soul, a study of the full counsel of God will help define the meaning. The Bible uses the word "soul" to describe a person or a living being to establish a body/soul relationship. Although distinctions are made, the word may refer to material substance or a spiritual entity. For many theologians the soul, being a spiritual entity, is said to consist of the mind, will, and emotions. [See Emotions; Mind; Will]

Sovereignty.   This refers to God's authority and power. God demonstrates His sovereignty through His omniscience, omnipotence, omnipresence and immutability. It affirms God's absolute, total authority and power. [See Omnipotent; Omniscience; Omnipresence; immutability]

Special Revelation. God reveals Himself as defined in the Bible and demonstrated through the person of Christ. [See Revelation]

Spontaneous actions. The thought in the 20th century is that choices proceed from neutral or equal desires. It states there is an effect without a cause. This however is impossible. [See Causality; Heisenberg principle]

Statism. This worldview assumes the secular government, also called the state, is the source of all provisions for its subjects. If taken to the logical end of its theory, the state is the source of salvation for those who belong to the state.

Stoicism. A system of philosophy that teaches self salvation through knowledge. This is pantheistic doctrine.

Subjectivistic hermeneutic. According to this doctrine everyone has their own interpretation of Scripture and all interpretations are equally valid. This is purely a relativistic hermeneutic which is not in keeping with the concept of the priesthood of the believer. [See Analogy of faith; Hermeneutics; Principle of private interpretation]

Subsistence. Calvin used this term to say that something stands under something else. He said there was an essential unity in the Godhead, but only one divine Being. The three persons of the Trinity subsist in the unity. [See Hypostasis]

Sui generis. (class of oneself) In theology it describes the "once-for-all-ness" of Jesus Christ. He was the ultimate final object and subject of biblical prophecy.

Summum bonum. (the highest good) A concept of the teleological ethic as people are confronted with goodness, wisdom, and power of God through his creation. [See Teleological ethic]

Supererogation. A term used in Roman Catholic doctrine to explain that one may receive more merit than is needed to enter into heaven. The extra merit goes into the treasury of merit. Christ plus the saints are said to have more merit than they need, so the surplus merit goes into the treasury of merit, to be distributed to others. A Roman view of substitutionary atonement wherein the substitute is not only Jesus Christ, but other men with more merit that they need for themselves to enter heaven. [See Treasury of merit]

Supralapsarianism. (From *supra* meaning above and *lapsus* meaning fall) The belief that God decreed election logically prior to His decree of the fall. It holds that God, wanting to show forth His wrath on some and His mercy on others, determined that He would decree the fall of man. Though the minority report historically among Reformed theologians, it nevertheless is within the mainstream of Reformed theology. Some estimates suggest that one third of the Westminster divines held this position while the other affirmed infralapsarianism, the view that God decreed the fall logically before the decrees of election and reprobation. Supralapsarian has the advantage of affirming that God decreed the fall for a reason. The disadvantage is that it seems to come close to making God unjust. [See Infralapsarianism]

Sustenance. God creates then He sustains His creation. He holds all things together. The universe and everything within it is dependent upon the being and power of God for continuity of existence as well as origin of existence. "For in him we live and move and have our being" (Acts 17:28). [See Providence]

Suzerain treaties. The kings of the Hittites would draw up official contracts called covenants with their vassal kings. The pattern was:

1) preamble
2) the historical prologue
3) stipulations
4) sanctions
5) ceremony of ratification including oaths and vows
6) provision of public reading.

The covenant between the two parties was binding until death. [See Covenant of grace]

Symmetrical view of predestination. In reference to predestination, God works in the same way with the reprobate and with the elect.

Syncretism. In biblical theology this refers to the Israelites adopting cultural practices and worship doctrine from other nations and religions. God gave His children a way of life and specific worship instructions. God commanded His children not to co-mingle any foreign religion with the true religion.

Synergism. (to work with) This describes a cooperative agreement between God and man so that the prevenient universal grace given to all men cooperates with God in the act of regeneration. [See Prevenient grace; Regeneration]

Synthesis. In Hegel's dialectical idealism the synthesis was the final step in resolving a contradiction. His thesis and resulting antithesis produces a synthesis. [See dialectic; dialectical idealism; Hegel]

Systematic theology.   The science of systematizing or ordering Biblical truth. Theology is spiritual, devotional, and existential. The goal of theology is to understand the nature and character of God and the condition of man based on the full counsel of God. [See Theology]

Taxonomy.   The science of classification and root of all science. It involves grouping things by categories involving the laws and principles of classification. God gave Adam the right to name the animals thus giving him authority over them thus making Adam the first taxonomist.

Te absolvo.   (I absolve you) In the Roman Catholic Church this action by the priest is granted to the one receiving the sacrament of penance. [See Penance]

Teleological argument.   This is one of several tools used by the classical apologist to prove theism.   It is the argument from design thus an intelligent designer of all of creation. [See Apologetics; Telos; Teleology]

Teleological ethics.   (teleological from the Greek word *telos*, refers to the end or final result of something and *logos* refers to the study of something) This theory in ethics teaches that the end or final result of an act determines whether an act is good or evil. This is often associated with the old saying "The end justifies the means."

Teleology.   The science of purpose, ends, goals or order. Relates to order and apparent design of the universe. Design presupposes a designer with intelligent purpose. The teleological argument is used as an argument for the existence of God. [See Telos; Teleological argument]

Telos. A Greek word meaning end, goal, or purpose. Jesus uses this word (verb form) in John 19:30: "it is finished" to indicate he accomplished his purpose. [See Teleology]

Temporal priority. A term used to describe the order of time in *ordo salutis* (order of salvation). It deals with the sequence of God's saving grace rather than the logic of God's saving grace. [See *Ordo salutis*]

Tetragrammaton. The four consonants YHWH forming the Hebrew incommunicable name of the Supreme Being which is translated "I AM WHO I AM." The Israelites replaced the word *Yahweh* with *Adonai* (both names translate to English as Lord) because they believed *Yahweh* was too sacred and therefore unapproachable with a common word.

Thales. He was recognized as the first Greek philosopher. He dealt with the relationship of the one to the many and the problem of diversity and unity. He wanted to find something that would give unity to the universe and he concluded that water was the unifying factor.

Theantrophic nature. (from the Greek words *theos* translated God and *anthropos* translated man combined into one word *theantrophic* refers to divine and human in one nature) A heresy wherein the human and divine natures of Jesus Christ were combined. This was the view of Eutyches. [See Monophysite heresy; Eutyches]

Theism. (derived from the Greek word *theos* meaning God and "ism" which is a noun forming suffix explaining concepts and conditions) Theism is a common term used to describe the triune God of Christianity. It defines God as the only source of being, creation, and salvation. It stands in opposition to atheism which says there is no god and polytheism which says there are many gods and deism which states that God is not active in the providential care of this world. [See Deism]

Theocentric.   (God at the center) This describes God's position in relation to creation. God is the only independent being, thus God is the center of all dependent creation. This term stands in stark contrast to anthropocentric (man is the center). Christians recognize God is the center of all of faith, life, and worship.

Theodicy.   (derived from the Greek word *theos* meaning God and *dike* meaning justice) The term itself is attributed to the 18th century philosopher Leibniz. The term literally means "the justice of God." It is used in debates over the origin of evil and free will. [See Achilles Heel of Christianity]

Theological liberalism.   Any theological system that modifies or denies the orthodox doctrine of the Christian Church. There are various levels of deviation from Christian orthodoxy, therefore care must be taken to analyze their doctrine. Theological liberalism is un-Christian because it denies the fundamentals of the faith like the virgin birth and bodily resurrection. The optimistic views of the 19th and 20th century liberals have failed to create a society of loving Christians. The result is the emptiness of the liberal message in a postmodern world. Historically, there are several lessons to be remembered about theological liberals.

1. They take conservative creeds and redefine them
2. They speak with slippery language
3. Their strategy is to take over schools

4. They refuse to listen to conservative scholarship.
[See Heresy; Orthodoxy]

Theology. This word means "a study of God." The broader sense of the word encompasses several theological disciplines such as: Systematic theology, Biblical theology, and Historical theology. Systematic theology attempts to organize the full corpus of God's revelation in this volume. Biblical theology deals with historical and redemptive aspects of theology as they are found in Scripture. Historical theology is the study of the development of the history of Christian doctrine.

Theonomy. The belief that all of God's law, save those ceremonial laws which are fulfilled in Christ, remains binding on the world, both individually and corporately. The distinctive element on this view is the belief that the Old Testament civil law, often called the judicial laws or the law code God established for Israel, ought to be the law of the land everywhere. Though theonomists claim a long heritage in the Reformed tradition, this view began to spread in Reformed circles in the 1970's principally thought the work of R. J. Rushdonny. [See Reconstructionism]

Theophany. An external visible manifestation of the invisible God. It is the appearance of God to man either through angelic or human beings. It may also be said that some appearances such as the "smoking oven and a burning torch" in Genesis 15:17 when God passed through the carcasses of the divided animals were *theophanies*.

Theosophy. The Greek word *theosophia* literally means "knowledge of God." Most often this term is associated with eastern religions that seek to unify all existence into one.

Thesis. In Hegel's dialectical idealism, the thesis is an existing idea or proposition. [See Hegel; Dialectical idealism]

Thomism.   The school of thought named for the great medieval Roman Catholic theologian, Thomas Aquinas (born 1225, died 1274). While Aquinas wrote philosophically and systematically, his two most enduring contributions were on the relationship between the sacred and the secular and especially his work on apologetics. Aquinas formulated the five classic arguments for God's existence:

1) the argument from motion,
2) from effects to a First Cause,
3) from contingent to Necessary Being,
4) from degrees of perfection to a Most Perfect Being,
5) the argument from design.

Thomas has been both praised and criticized for combining elements of Christian thought with Aristotelian thought.

Total depravity.   This describes how original sin has corrupted and defiled every aspect of the human being. The mind, emotions, and will are corrupted as a result of the sin of Adam and Eve. Paul the Apostle describes the condition of the human race as being dead in trespasses and sins (Ephesians 2:1), inexcusable (Romans 2:1), and under the condemnation of death (1 Corinthians 15:21). [See Original sin]

Totaliter aliter.   (totally other) This was the view of Karl Barth that God is wholly other than man and therefore cannot communicate with man. [See Barth, Karl; Wholly other]

Traducianist.   The doctrine that teaches the human soul is transmitted to the child from the parents. This opposes the view of the creation of the soul *ex nihilo*. [See Creation ex nihilo]

Transcendent. Christian theology uses this term to mean that God is higher than the created universe. He is the only Being who is self existent. He is the only One with the power of Being within Himself. [See Aseity]

Treasury of merit. The Roman Catholic Church teaches that surplus merit can be transferred to persons deficient in merit. [See Supererogation]

Trent. [See Council of Trent]

Trinity. This is one of the fundamental tenets of the Christian religion. This doctrine teaches the unity of the Father, Son, and Holy Spirit in one Divine nature. The *Westminster Shorter Catechism* teaches that "the three (Father, Son, and Holy Spirit) are the same in substance, equal in power and glory." Although the word Trinity is not found in Scripture, by inference it is abundantly and manifestly taught in Scripture. Sometimes the term "economic trinity" may be used to refer to distinct functions that ultimately separate their personalities. This is contrary to the doctrine explained by the Westminster divines and other reformed theologians. [See Compound being; Hypostasis; Simple being]

Tripartite view of man. This teaches that man has a body, soul, and spirit. It is generally used to support various views on sanctification. Classical Christianity rejected this view until the 20th century, but is now accepted by some corners of dispensationalism and neo-Pentecostalism. [See Soul]

Truth. Objective reality verifiable to the mind with at least three levels of understanding.
1) Awareness of truth – A function of the mind.
2) Conviction of truth – A function of the will.

3) Conscience - The conviction becomes so strong it reaches the conscience.

Ubiquity. (equal whereness) This concept describes that God is fully present everywhere. In Roman Catholic doctrine it is said that Jesus Christ in his human nature can be everwhere at once. [See Omnipresence]

Ubiquity controversy. This refers to the communication of attributes especially through the human nature of Christ. This was an argument between Luther and Calvin in relationship to the sacrament of the Lord's Supper. [See Hoc est corpus meun; Ubiquity]

Unconditional election. This Calvinistic doctrine teaches that election is not based on any condition of merit in men, or God's foreknowledge of who would come to faith. A simple clarification is that eternal salvation is not conditioned on man's ability to save himself, thus the use of the term "unconditional."

Ungodliness. This word is used in connection with Romans one to describe the condition of man. Man's nature is contrary to God's nature in that man is without the holy character of God, inclined to do evil until the Holy Spirit changes the heart to believe the gospel and trust Christ for eternal life. [See Unright-eousness; Sin]

Universalism. This doctrine teaches that any future punish-ment is designed to purge the sins of people so that in the end everyone will be saved. [See Atonement]

University. The concept of the university captured the combination of unity and diversity in the quest for education in the Middle ages. Theology, the queen of sciences, was the primary instrument used to pursue an understanding of unity in a diverse world. The university today is merely a school of higher learning where people go to learn a trade or profession to produce more income during the lifetime. Eliminating theology in the university takes away the only discipline that seeks to understand reality. [See Queen of the Sciences]

Unrighteousness. A general statement about man's evil condition found in Romans 1:18. [See Ungodliness; Sin]

Utter depravity. This term must be distinguished from total depravity. It describes the condition of human beings as being as evil as they can possibly be. This is not taught in the Bible and would cause the annihilation of the human race. [See Total depravity]

Vaticinia ex eventu. A future prediction after the event has already occurred. This was Bultmann's concept of biblical prophecy.

Venial sin. The Roman Catholic Church teaches that this sin is real, but not serious enough to kill justifying grace in the soul.

Vernacular Bible. Martin Luther popularized the Bible by putting it into the most common mode of expressing language (German) for the German people. The Bible ought to be translated into every language.

Verification principle. This term is used in conjunction with Logical Positivism which teaches that no statement or proposition is meaningful unless it can be verified empirically. [See Logical Positivism]

Verbum dei. (the word of God) Calvin referred to this as the inspired word of Holy Scripture.

Via eminentia. (The way of eminence) The way of understanding divine attributes by raising attributes of things in the finite order. For example, men have power, but God has all power. A term used in process theology. [See Panentheism; Process theology]

Via negationis. (the way of negation) Sometime we define something by saying what it is not. A method of defining the divine attributes by negating the attributes of the finite order. For example, creatures are measurable, but God is immeasurable. A term used in process theology. [See Panentheism; Process theology]

Vorverstandis. (prior understanding) This is Bultmann's new hermeneutic whereby one must come to Scripture with that prior understanding. [See Bultmann's new hermeneutic]

Vox dei.   (the voice of God) Calvin referred to this as the Word of God but not inerrant or infallible. Calvin said, "among the many excellent gifts with which God has adorned the human race, it is a singular privilege that he deigns to consecrate to himself the mouths and tongues of men in order that his voice may resound in them." (*Institutes of the Christian Religion* 4.1.5)

Warfield, B. B. (1851-1921) The last great theologian of the conservative Presbyterians at Princeton. He did not believe that total depravity destroyed man's ability to reason. His classical apologetics are a tribute to his life long study of the Word of God.

Wartburg Castle.   After the Diet of Worms, Luther was taken there by friends for his own protection. It was there that

Luther translated the Bible into German for the common people.

Wholly other. Karl Barth believed that God was wholly other from man. Implied that if God was wholly other, God cannot communicate with man. [See Barth, Karl; Totaliter aliter]

Will. This aspect of the soul is that part that makes decisions relative to conditions and contingencies associated with the thinking mind. The will of God is perfect unlike the will of sinful man. Volition is the act of choice according to the prevailing good that comes from the result of the choice. [See Freedom of the will; Soul]

Works of satisfaction. This was the crux of the 16th century Reformation. The Roman Catholic Church taught that these works are produced by doing good works. It changes the biblical doctrine of repentance.

Postmodern Words

One of the most profound words in the English language is "why?"

Children often use the why question to learn. For instance, a young child might ask his father or mother a question about the reality of birds.

Question: Daddy, why do birds fly?
Answer: Because they have wings.

Question: Why do birds have wings?
Answer: Because God made them with wings.

Question: Why did God make them with wings?
Answer: For God's own glory.

Question: Why did God make them for His own glory?
Answer: Because He did. Now go out and play.

The question "why" is profound because it has to do with purpose. There must be purpose for every human thought or action. Purpose is the driving force behind human existence. Purpose is behind every decision. A child attempts to understand reality by asking questions. How much more should adults try to understand reality? Your choice follows your purpose. There is no in between. Jesus said, "He who is not with me is against me" (Matthew 12:30). Neutrality is not optional for those who have purpose.

Neutrality is the phantom of egalitarianism. No society can be neutral and therefore egalitarianism is nothing more than the tyranny of a dysfunctional culture. The cultural war zones produced by the words of postmodernity are proof that neutrality is impossible and egalitarianism is nothing but a front for those tyrants who want to micro-manage society. The cultural wars are fought on the battleground of the public arena. They are the battles fought over the family, art, education, law, politics, and interpretative theory. The clash began at the point when different people had different ideas about reality. The dispute is not over philosophical ideals. Quite to the contrary, the dispute is over words that establish philosophical ideas. For instance, the abortion issue is not a cultural war, per se. Neo-Christian ethicists, liberal politicians and judges are on one side of the abortion issue. Conservative Christians, the right to life movement, and orthodox ethicists are on the other side of the abortion issue. Abortion is the catalyst that the cultural elites use to determine who controls the family, the court system, the political arena and the education of children. These cultural wars are fought over authority and control. Where there is a question of authority, neutrality is not possible.

The attempt to define the American culture has not been an easy road to travel. Each generation tries to re-define the cultural milieu of the previous generation. The argument is that culture is relative to people and circumstances. Opening the doors to cultural relativity was the beginning of the cultural wars in this country. Although we speak of these cultural wars in terms of the mid-twentieth century, they have always visited us in one form or the other.

The American culture has never been free from debates in the public arena; nor should it ever be. The polarization of society demands intelligent discourse to resolve division when two parties maintain different sentiments. The process of intellectual discourse is by means of debate or disputation. It is never wise to concede to the old pseudo-peace slogan, "Let's agree to disagree." However, the debates need a solid foundation, because real debates are concerned only about reality. The only solid foundation for reality must be metaphysical. Rational beings must look beyond this physical world if they expect to understand the world around them, the world they most commonly call culture.

Since every word has ultimate purpose, definitions are not merely important, they are necessary for intelligent discussion. For instance, the word metaphysical must be defined before it is used in intellectual discussion. Metaphysics refers to questions of ultimate reality and ultimate reality takes us to the intellectual, moral, and emotional aspect of our being. Metaphysical reality is the source of ultimate purpose. The proximate purposes such as the bird having to have wings to fly is evidence for ultimate purpose.

Rational people understand human suffering because they have experienced it, witnessed it, or read about it. People killing each other and destruction of property is as common as eating a meal. For those who miss the malicious suffering, there is hedonism, narcissism, and a whole host of other worldviews that lead to uncertainty. For many there is a sense of emptiness, because there is no understanding of ultimate purpose. Many of the theologians, philosophers, and political theorists of the puritan era understood proximate purpose and that purpose was built upon the solid foundation of metaphysical purpose. Jonathan Edwards explained this concept in Freedom of the Will. "We can have no proof, that is properly demonstrative, of any one proposition, relating to the being and nature of God, his creation of the world, the dependence of all things on him, the nature of bodies or spirits, the nature of our own souls, or any of the great truths of morality and natural religion but what is metaphysical" (*Freedom of the Will*, Yale Edition, by Jonathan Edwards, p. 424).

There remains the hope to recover that metaphysical reality because there was and remains purpose behind the concept. I am convinced that without any metaphysical inquiry and without substantial agreement because of the inquiry, Christianity will diminish and the neutrality of the postmodern world will emerge. If a culture is not built on a sound foundation, it like any other edifice, the pilings will rot away.

If we place the political and social aspects of a culture on a continuum, we might have two extremes: Cultural tyranny on one end or cultural anarchy on the other end. Those two extremes have given rise to the postmodern state. Modernity was very happy to fight over cultural issues such as education, politics or the family, so long as the gathered rational data or the scientific method could be used to measure the result of the battle. However, the cultural anarchist could not agree with the cultural tyrant over the results of the test. For instance, one educator we will call the cultural tyrant may desire for you to turn your children completely over to the educational system. Those educators, who are not educators at all, want to shape the children into social engineers, rather than educate them to become productive thinking citizens. Another educator, we will call the cultural anarchist, has no interest in the education of the child. Those types of educators, who are not educators at all, have no agenda to produce intelligent productive citizens. Wherever the cultural battle is fought, we see the myth of neutrality and no solid foundation upon which to build cultural norms.

Metaphysical neutrality has brought the American culture to a new crossroads. The postmodern culture will have nothing to do with the alleged absolutes of modernity. Philosophers talk about "the emptiness of the modern mind" because modernity failed to meet those world and life views with answers that satisfied the soul of the culture. If urbanization, capitalism and technology, especially technology, failed to shape the culture, then the postmodernist would say, what is the purpose of modernity? The blighted hope of the modern failure finds comfort, strange as that may seem, in the postmodern culture.

Individual expressions of truth to the postmodern mind are simply nonsensical, especially since the postmodern rejects absolute truth. The result is we have a truth neutral culture. There is no metaphysic and neutrality has been crowned king.

Objective definitions are the foundation for political institutions, moral discussions, social practices and economic debate. Without objective definitions, the culture will continue its endless drift through a maze of destructive ideas.

The postmodernist will tell you that all you have to do is redefine your terms. The postmodern interpretive theory attempts to neutralize terms. Postmodern interpretive theory is in a nascent state. It is like the embryo about to emerge into new life in the world. Richard Tarnas explains the postmodern interpretative theory. "No interpretation of a text can claim decisive authority because that which is being interpreted inevitably contains hidden contradictions that undermine its coherence. Hence all meaning is ultimately undecidable, and there is no 'true' meaning. No underlying primal reality can be said to provide the foundation for human attempts to represent truth. Texts refer only to other texts, in an infinite regress, with no secure basis in something external to language" (*The Passion of the Western Mind*, by Richard Tarnas, p. 399). We have already seen what this interpretative twist has done to the literary world, but can you imagine what will happen to historical interpretation in the generations to come. In the postmodern understanding, interpretation is everything; reality only comes into being through our interpretations of what the world means to us individually. Postmodernism relies on human experience over abstract principles, knowing always that the outcome of one's own experience will necessarily be fallible and relative, rather than certain and universal. Postmodern words will take the American culture into a neo-dark age.

About the Author

Martin Murphy has a B.A. in Bible from Columbia International University and Master of Divinity from Reformed Theological Seminary. Martin spent nearly thirty years in the class room, the pulpit, the lectern, the study, and the library. He now devotes most of his time consolidating academic and practical gains by writing books. He is the author of fourteen books. He and his wife live in Dothan, Alabama.

The Church: First Thirty Years, 344 pages, ISBN 9780985618179, $15.95. This book is an exposition of the Book of Acts. It will help Christians understand the purpose, mission, and ministry of the church.

The Dominant Culture: Living in the Promised Land, 172 pages, ISBN 970991481118, $11.95. This book examines the culture of Israel during the period of the Judges. It explains how worldviews influence the church and it reveals biblical principles to help Christians learn how to live in the culture.

My Christian Apology, 98 pages, ISBN 9780984570874, $7.95. This book investigates the doctrine of Christian apologetics. It explains rational Christian apologetics.

The Essence of Christian Doctrine, 200 pages, ISBN 9780984570812, $12.95. This book was written so that pastors and laymen would have a quick reference to major biblical doctrines. Dr. Steve Brown says it was written, "with clarity and power about the verities of the Christian faith and in a way that makes a difference in how we live."

Hosea Commentary: Return to the Lord, 130 pages, ISBN 9780998560601, $7.95. This book is an exposition of Hosea. The prophet speaks a message of repentance and hope. Hosea's prophetic message to Old Testament and New Testament congregations is, "you have broken God's covenant; return to the Lord." Dr. Richard Pratt said, "We need more correct and practical instruction in the prophetic books, and you have given us just that."

Brief Study of the Ten Commandments, 164 pages, 9780991481163, $10.95. This book will help Christians discover or re-discover the meaning of the Ten Commandments.

The Present Truth, 164 pages, ISBN 9780983244172, $8.95. Each chapter examines a topic relative to the Christian life. Topics such as church, sin, anger, marriage, education and more.

Doctrine of Sound Words: Summary of Christian Theology, 423 pages, ISBN 9780991481125, $16.95. This is a book of Christian doctrine in topical format. It covers a wide range of theological topics such as, the triune God, creation, providence, sin, justification, repentance, Christian liberty, free will, marriage and divorce, Christian fellowship, et al). There are thirty three topics beginning with "Holy Scriptures" and ending with "The Last Judgment." It is a systematic theology for laymen based on the full counsel of God.

Friendship: The Joy of Relationships, ISBN 9780986405518, 48 pages, $6.49 . This is the kind of book that friends give each other and share the principles with each other. If friends do not feel comfortable sharing these relationship principles with each other, the friendship may not really exist. Friendship involves a relationship of distinction. It is a relationship that respects the dignity of another person. The Bible teaches a different version of what it means to be a friend than the popular culture teaches.

There are many occasions when friends say they are friends, but they are not friends. "Even my own familiar friend in whom I trusted, who ate my bread, has lifted up his heel against me" (Psalm 41:9). A true friend will endure and sacrifice for a friend. "A friend loves at all times" (Proverbs 17:7) and "there is a friend who sticks closer than a brother" (Proverbs 18:24).

Ultimate Authority for the Soul, 151 pages, ISBN 9780986405501, $9.99
This book examines that question and concludes that every rational being has some recognition of God as the ultimate authority. Although God is the ultimate authority, He confers His authority by means of the Word of God. The author examines Psalm 119 to build a defense for the ultimate authority for the soul.

Constitutional Authority in a Postmodern Culture, ISBN 9780985618124, 56 pages, $5.95
This book shows the validity of constitutional authority and the invasion of postmodern theories in western culture. Postmodern theory has assaulted the western culture on the battleground of absolute truth and reality. Postmodern theory places human experience over abstract objective principles. Christians have a constitution known as the Bible so they will know the truth of reality. The last chapter is devoted to cultural reformation.

Learn to Pray: Biblical Doctrine of Prayer, ISBN 9780986405563, 107 pages, $7.95.
This book examines the Lord's model prayer so Christians may learn to pray according to the Lord's instruction. It also reviews some of the prayers of the apostle Paul to discover his doctrine of prayer. Pastor James Perry wrote the Foreword with insight and experience. "I am impressed with this book on the subject of Learn to Pray. It is stated briefly and succinctly following

the model and example of the Lord's Prayer. There is consider-
able practical instruction on the meaning and implication about
purposeful and biblical prayer and it will serve as a useful
primer for all who apply the prayer principles. The reader will
doubtlessly return to the instruction frequently for the practical
help it offers."

The god of the Church Growth Movement, 95 pages ISBN
9781448655243
This work includes a brief explanation of modernity and its
effect on church growth. It is a critical analysis of the church
growth movement found in every branch of the Protestant
church.

Printed in Great Britain
by Amazon

37865892R00076